OSBORN HOME LIBRARY
RYE, NEW YORK

This book commemorates

the gift of

Mrs. Hazel Bird

D1229881

CALL IT A SUMMER COUNTRY

CALL IT A SUMMER COUNTRY

Signed for Mrs Hazel Bird
who loves Fotheringhay
as much as

EDWARD STOREY

Edward Storey

Photographs by
John Baguley

John Baguley.

ROBERT HALE · LONDON

ISBN 0 7091 7103 X

Robert Hale Limited
Clerkenwell House
Clerkenwell Green
London, EC1

Photoset by Bristol Typesetting Co. Ltd.,
and printed in Great Britain by
Lowe & Brydone Ltd., Thetford, Norfolk

Contents

Acknowledgements

In addition to those thanked specially in my introduction I would also like to acknowledge my gratitude to the Dean and Chapter of Peterborough Cathedral; the American Battle Monuments Commission; the Nature Conservancy; the Estate of the late Dr Alfred Noyes and to William Blackwood & Sons Ltd, for permission to quote so liberally from " The Burial of a Queen "; and to the Estate of Robert Frost and Jonathan Cape Ltd, for permission to print " Reluctance ".

Illustrations

To my brothers and sister
who shared part
and must believe the rest

" Whoever has travelled Great Britain before us, and whatever they have written, tho' they may have had a harvest, yet they have always passed over so much that others may come and glean after them by large handfuls . . ."

Defoe

Introduction

" Why do you always write about winter?" asked a friendly critic after the publication of one of my books.

Well, I didn't realize that I was so single-minded, and yet, on looking at some of my earlier titles and dust-jackets, perhaps he had a just reason for making his comment.

It's true I have written a lot about winter; I was born in winter; I have a weakness for winter landscapes in paintings; and there is something cosy about closing the shutters early in the evening and sitting by the fire while the frost or snow happens outside.

But surely, I thought, I'm not all that one-sided, not just a one-season man? Admittedly the individual quality or character of the fen country, its remoteness, bleakness, stillness, and certain aloofness, always appear more dramatic in winter; but the fens, too, have their warmer, more romantic seasons and they can be as beguiling in July and August as they are frightening in December or January.

" So why not write about the fens next time," my critic might have said, " and call this part of England *a summer country* for a change!"

To be sure, the idea appealed to me straightaway because I do also like summer. I like warm, lazy days. I like summer landscapes of harvest-fields and heavy fruit trees, of seashores and holiday-makers. But, if confession is good for the soul, I have to admit that for a couple of years I have been trying *not* to write about the fens at all. I suppose I was afraid of some less friendly critic saying. " How long is it before a furrow becomes a rut?" And, like many another writer, I had notions about writing several different kinds of books—plays, novels and so on—if only to convince myself, in some small measure, of my own versatility. But those ideas didn't amount to very much and the promised words remained unborn. Instead of travelling through a world of exotic places, and writing about all kinds of different people, I found myself in something like a desert, a strange kind of wilderness where nothing much happened. My small workroom became a prison where words did not blossom but stared at me like stones, defiant and dead.

Perhaps I was the one being defiant, turning my back on the obvious, on the land that had been so generous in the past. " You write about those things you know and love best " is the advice often given to young writers, and I should have realized that I couldn't work when I was deliberately trying to cut my imagination off from its natural food supply, from the landscape and people which have nurtured it for many years. So I left my desk one morning and went out again into that landscape where I have so often found myself—

I went out because I could not ignore the season
For too long I tried to disown the throb of earth's blood.
But today, driving against my will, it came back—
The old pulse, the inevitable surrender to skies and mist.

Baled hay stood dry and grey as abbey ruins—grass
Cloisters through which the shadows of dead men passed.
A lark sang and the river recorded its notes on a tape
of water to play back one day in the memory.

For a moment I felt that the earth reproached me.
So I said " Forgive me that I should have grown so proud,
What am I without you? " And the mist moved away
Leaving the fields shining innocently under the sun.

My heart and mind were, indeed, both grateful for the reconciliation and acceptance, and the memory was soon alive with those warm days recorded long ago, or not too distantly experienced. I knew also that there were other warm days soon to be lived, another summer to be shared, and slowly the words began to breathe and have life.

Now, having admitted that I have returned to the subject of the fen country for my writing I must also say that this is not going to be just another book about the fens. They will, naturally, be seen as a major part of the summer landscape about which I write, but in writing about that landscape I have also been able to feature places that are not even in the fen country. This has been done by looking at the three main fenland rivers from their source—the Great Ouse, the Nene, and the Welland, on whose banks are such interesting places as Godmanchester, St Ives, Oundle, Fotheringhay, Rockingham and Stamford.

During this summer, which I like to see as an epitome, or concentration, of summers, there have also been weeks spent in Cambridge, days in Norfolk and Lincolnshire, visits to nature reserves, and hours of conversation with people who have spent a lifetime in their own special corner of East Anglia—farm-workers, horse-keepers, reserve wardens and artists—people with a long experience of all the seasons that this part of England offers year after year.

I have also been able to look at this countryside from totally different and unfamiliar aspects—from the River Ouse, for instance, on which I spent a few days observing the landscape from the water. Several people have helped me too to look deeper into the reasons for this countryside's particular characteristics, and I am grateful to them.

Someone said to me only the other day, " As you get older summer becomes more than just a season. It's a period of life, rich in its own memories and other associations." Certainly in writing this book I have found some truth in those words. I have been reminded many times of other summers and begin to measure each one by the memories of those long gone so that, even though 1976 was officially the hottest summer on record, I'm quite prepared to accept the argument of one old man who said: "I *know* there were hotter summers in my childhood because I can remember the tar on the roads melting and running like rain-water down the street."

Well, you can't contradict a memory like that. For that old man of eighty-four there never could be a summer hotter than that of his childhood when life, and roads, and perhaps even tar were different. I too look back to summers that I'm sure were warmer than any I have known recently or will know in future; and why should I consult the records to disillusion myself? After all, *this* summer, or next, could well be, in years to come, the one that I shall look back on with a romantic degree of affection, but it may not be the hottest summer, or the best summer according to the Met. Office, and it's unlikely, I think, to surpass those childhood summers at Hunstanton or Great Yarmouth when the sun blistered my shoulders and grilled my spine.

My own childhood was spent in the nineteen-thirties but,

despite all the gloom that was around in the world then, those summers remain in my memory as some of the happiest days of my life and I have not been able to resist some mention of them. Time has, I'm sure, enhanced those memories, as it enhances most of childhood, but I have been reminded of them frequently as I lazed in the heat of a modern summer, smelling again the half-forgotten smells of a dusty garden-path that is no longer there; the drooping nettles near an apple-tree that fell down aeons ago; a patch of horse-radish whose pungency still fills the air; the dark stillness of rain captured in our water-butt; the dolly-tub full of soap-suds on Monday morning wash-days; the fields, festivals, games and seaside-outings that are as alive now as they ever were.

Yes, I know that childhood summers are like childhood Christmases that simmer slowly in the quieter corners of the mind year after year, maturing like a heady wine, slowly growing their own hazy legends of how things *used* to be. I know, too, that if we were transported back to the brutal truths of reality we would be in for a saddening shock. Thankfully the Past is past and we simply enjoy the privilege of making of it what we wish. If our memories want to indulge again and again in all the joys, gifts, heat-waves, good times and innocence of long ago, then why not let the memory have its own holiday. Summer is, after all, a time for harvest, for reaping and storing.

This book, then, is about the past and the present, about the fens and the surrounding countryside, about the different events that have gone into making our own season that much richer and, I hope, memorable. You cannot spend a summer in Cambridge, Huntingdon, St Ives, Godmanchester, Fothering-hay, King's Lynn or Hunstanton without thinking about the past because they are places full of history—national and personal, significant and private. You cannot sit by a river with-out giving some thought to the waters that have already reached the sea. And you cannot travel through this part of the country without giving some consideration to people like Mary Queen of Scots, Oliver Cromwell, William Cowper, George Borrow, John Clare, and several other distinguished natives or residents.

I have deliberately tried not to write about too many churches because they do get written about rather a lot in other and more formal guides, but a few have rightly claimed some attention, gaining a little perhaps in being selected. I realize too that there will appear to be several omissions of places and events that would normally find their way into a book on such a diverse area. This is mainly because I have written about them in earlier volumes and did not want to repeat myself unnecessarily in this. King's Lynn, Spalding, Wisbech, Ely and Cambridge could all have been given much more space here, so too could the story of fen drainage, agriculture, industry, and the traditional pursuits of the fenman —shooting and ice-skating. I am equally aware that a writer like John Clare should have been given much more room in a book which covers much of his own landscape for he is undoubtedly a "poet of place", but again I have already written about Clare in previous publications and have there-fore resisted the temptation to say more than I felt particularly relevant in some of the following pages. Where I have thought that some reference to one of my earlier works was needed I have run the risk of being considered immodest by mentioning the appropriate title.

I trust, then, that the thoughts, impressions and remi-niscences that you find in these chapters will help you to appreciate the character and atmosphere of this summer country, that perhaps my words will help to enhance an afternoon spent in this part of England where the wheat ripens as you watch, where the days drift cloudlike over quiet fields, and the rivers flow gently to the sea with their invisible cargoes of your own contented hours.

For me the summer, and this book, would not have been possible without the experience and memories of people like Mrs Ivy Dow; Mr Sam Briggs; Mr Gordon Mason; Mr Geoffrey Armstrong; and Mr Wilfred Leonard. I would also like to express my gratitude to Mr George Dixon (for intro-ducing me to *Tales of the Mermaid Tavern* by Alfred Noyes): John and Doreen Lewis for their ideas and encouragement; Mr Rod Stratford and the sixth-form pupils at Hinchingbrooke House; Miss Mary Liquorice of Peterborough Central Library; and Mr John Baguley, the photographer, who patiently pursued some of the shots I particularly wanted for this book. There are others who deserve thanks but they are strangers who shared an hour with me here or there and disappeared, nameless, unknown, and unaware that they had contributed something to my work.

E.S.

I

Protected Worlds

Early morning; the mist still loitering slowly, silently between trees and buildings, like a tired nightwatchman reluctant to go home.

I have recently moved into an old house in the cathedral precincts at Peterborough and my windows look out on to the not inconspicuous west front of that impressive building, an architectural wonder praised by John Ruskin and photographed by millions of visitors ever since the camera was invented.

The cathedral is still closed. The daily services have not yet begun. I get the feeling that I am the only person awake, but in saying that I am perhaps being unfair to my neighbours.

This room will be the starting point of most of my summer excursions and explorations into the countryside of Cambridgeshire, Lincolnshire and Norfolk. Within this quietness I hope I shall be able to reflect upon the impressions that each day yields.

On one of my window-panes is scratched the name and date of a previous tenant who lived here in 1886. The house was already 160 years old then and it's a reassuring thought, so early in the morning, to know that over the years quite a few pairs of eyes have looked out on a scene that has changed very little during the centuries since the cathedral was built.

Certainly it is very difficult to convince myself that I am in fact living in the second half of the twentieth century. No one is about in clothes that would appear strange to earlier dwellers. No cars have arrived—yet. No men with briefcases, or women with shopping trolleys. The grass is only just beginning to wake up. The daisies have not stirred themselves. The lime trees are holding their breath above the permanent shadows that they dripped yesterday on to the ground below.

I look again at the great building that has dominated this view for nearly 900 years. Familiarity does not lessen its impact. This morning, in this early summer mist, you get the feeling that anything from its long history could happen. It competes with the silence. The silence withstands it. Mist and stone wait for the first sound. It could be the solemn beat of a muffled drum as the funeral cortège of Catherine of Aragon, or Mary Queen of Scots, arrives; it could be the fanfare for the arrival of a living monarch; or the triumphant sound of an anthem welcoming a new bishop. Such occasions have happened—Henry III, Edward I, Edward III, and Elizabeth II, to name but a few. But today it is more likely to be the sound of the verger turning his key in the iron gates and sighing at the thought of another day's work.

I wait . . . and then the first bird tentatively tries out his song. He gains confidence and keeps going. Others join in. The lime trees tremble and stretch their arms a little. The mist finally shuffles away.

I never thought that I would ever be so much in love with the day's beginning, but I am. I even begin to regret that I have been a nocturnal creature for so long and have missed so many dawns.

To be part of first light, to share in the first sounds of the day's unfolding, is, I have lately discovered, an extra blessing in life. As well as stars and midnight I now praise birdsong and milkmen. I can get up and make a cup of tea against the background of the dawn chorus. I can have breakfast before the sun clears the tree-tops and before the first cars arrive. I can walk in the bright and empty streets and feel as unique as Adam— well, almost! My only living competitor is the newsagent frantically untying his bundles of bad news.

I've decided that midday is plenty soon enough to read the newspaper. Why litter the mind's path with sensational headlines? Let it enjoy the freshness and the stillness of the morning. By all means bid the newsagent a good-day, but then pass on and leave him with his pile of world-shattering stories, Stock Exchange prices, provocative pin-ups and political scandals.

What, I ask myself with a mild curiosity, would have been some of the headlines that my previous tenants would have seen in their morning papers? 1759—Wolfe Defeats the French at Quebec. 1789—Mr. George Washington Elected First President of the U.S.A. 1812—Napoleon Retreats from Moscow. 1813—Slavery to be Abolished Throughout British

Empire. 1869—Suez Canal Opened. 1895—Marconi Sends First Wireless Message Over One Mile. 1903—Man Conquers Flight.

Ah well, the headlines are different now I suppose because the world is different. Or is it? In some things, maybe. In another hundred, or two hundred, years' time, these windows will have looked out over many more historical events, and this room's new tenants will have read the headlines of their own times, and ours: Man Conquers Everest; Man Conquers Space; Man Lands on the Moon; Human Heart Transplants; President Kennedy Assassinated; Race Riots; U.S.A. Manufactures Neutron Bomb.

But the news can wait. The stones and the mist have seen it all before. So too has the river. If only the stones could speak, or the water be played back. In some ways perhaps they can. In their stillness they say "Listen, and we will tell you!"

*   *   *

This morning the River Nene is quiet and belongs to summer. The water has flowed through meadows, parklands and villages rich with history and royal memories— like Fotheringhay, for instance, to which we shall return in the next chapter. Now it straightens out into the artificial course that Man has made for it to pass safely through the low fen country to the Wash. From the town bridge I look downstream. Birds and boats are reflected perfectly in the still water. Behind me a train crosses the railway bridge on its way to London. The first bus approaches the city bringing people in to their work.

It's an interesting thought that nearly everyone who has entered Peterborough from the south over the last 800 years has done so over a bridge that has crossed this stretch of the Nene; and there have not been that many bridges either during all that time.

One of the earliest bridges we know about was built in 1308 by the Abbot at a cost of just over £13. With a few extra supports and minor repairs this bridge survived until 1872 when it was replaced by an iron bridge which cost the town £5,500. But, by this time, the railways had also arrived and people entering the city then had not only to cross the water but also the railway lines that served the eastern counties. It worked for a while, when delays didn't seem to matter all that much, but the city was growing industrially and tempting more and more people in to work. So, by 1934, the old iron bridge over the river made way for a new stone bridge that now spans both water and rail.

* * *

The day is busy now and it's time for me to make my way out of the city to begin the first of my summer excursions into the surrounding countryside. There is no real plan, as yet; I tend to follow my nose.

Within minutes I find myself driving along the southbound carriageway of the A1. Freight lorries, almost as big as Westminster Abbey, overtake me and I feel momentarily intimidated.

The volume of traffic on this road is, at times, frightening; more frightening than any highwayman. Today, in a small car, you 'stand and deliver' without even being challenged. Headlights flash at me as threateningly as pistols. For a moment I wonder what I have done wrong until I realize that I am going too slow in the slow lane for some of the high-powered juggernauts thundering up behind me. I'll admit that I do have a habit of wanting to look out of my side-windows as well as the windscreen when I'm driving; fields can be so distracting, especially in summer; and you can't take them in at seventy miles an hour.

This section of the A1 is however only for my convenience and I escape the stampede to London by turning off into Sawtry Fen, park the car, and begin to walk the rough track that crosses the fen, away from the noise, into the past.

* * *

Peace! Within seconds the clamour and the chasing, the intimidation and the contest are all forgotten. I walk between the still, green crops and clusters of wild flowers. I can hear the rustling of cornstalks and the chatter of field birds.

Soon the historic associations of this landscape begin to have meaning and the names are no longer just words on a map. Only a short distance away once stood the abbey of Sawtry; an abbey which had a reputation for hard work and alms-giving. In an old rhyme about the fenland abbeys we read of the virtues of Ramsey, Thorney, Croyland, Spalding and Peter-borough, but

Sawtry, by the way, that old abbey
Gave more alms in one day than all they.

Now, alas, there is no more tangible evidence left to remind us of those good works; no empty nave; no broken columns or arches open to the sky; no visible signs of the cloisters and chapels of a religious community once famous for its industry and charity, a community of considerable influence in the fens.

There may be no abbey ruins but there are still one or two features in the landscape itself to remind us of the monks' labours here 800 years ago. Just beyond the main railway line that runs from London to the north is a canal known as Monks Lode. This canal is believed to have been dug by the monks in 1176 to help them get the stone from their quarry in Barnack, across the fens to their abbey site at Sawtry. They could get as far as the southern end of Whittlesea Mere by water but then had nearly four miles of heavy land to cross. There was only one answer—make it possible for the barges to go all the way. It was a brave and imaginative plan to cut a new canal through such difficult country in those days and it needed the blessing of Pope Alexander III before they could excavate on land which already belonged to Ramsey Abbey. Abbeys guarded their properties very jealously and frequently entered into long legal battles to keep what they possessed, or to add more. Having got the go-ahead from Rome it still needed a lot of back-breaking labour from someone to make this new waterway and, when one remembers the problems that Cornelius Vermuyden was to have with his labour-force 500 years later, the Sawtry monks' achievement is almost a miracle. Perhaps it was!

The amount of stone that left the Barnack quarries during the eleventh and twelfth centuries is quite phenomenal. Stone not only for Sawtry, Peterborough and Ramsey, but for Thorney, Lynn, Ely and Bury St Edmunds; stone which, incidentally, after the Dissolution went into all kinds of building in many different parts of the country, including stately homes and colleges. The handling and transport of such quantities, 800 years ago, must have been an enormous undertaking, causing a few sore shoulders as well as headaches.

Today, in this quiet agricultural scene, it is a test of the imagination's power to recreate those days of digging, barging, building, psalm-chanting and alms-giving.

Back on to the A1 for a moment and then quickly on to the B1090, signposted Woodwalton and Abbots Ripton.

I slow down and look around. The land undulates and is thickly clustered with trees. Indeed, it is one of the last areas where trees will predominate before entering the fen country for a while. We shall come to trees again in Norfolk but, between here and there, there will be a noticeable absence of any large area of trees. So I will breathe in the sweet smell of woodlands now, while I have the chance: Archers' Wood, Coppingford Wood, Upton Wood, Monks' Wood, Wennington Wood (worth seeing in spring for its bluebells), and, lastly, one of my favourite little woodlands—Woodwalton Nature Reserve.

Most of these woods once belonged to an ancient woodland that would have been continuous from west of Ermine Street almost to Ramsey. Many acres have disappeared but several of those that remain are ones that are mentioned in the Domesday Book.

The woods became separated in the thirteenth century when trees had to be cut back from the highway for the protection of travellers. An order was given in 1242 to John de Neville, bailiff of the King's forests, to cut a highway through Sawtry Wood, Coppingford Wood, and Upton Wood, " of sufficient width for the safety of travellers ", the recommended width being a bow-shot's length.

Monks' Wood is one of the best remaining examples of the original forest and belonged to a number of landowners even before it came into the possession of Sawtry Abbey. One of the earliest transactions is believed to be that between King Canute and Turkill of Harringworth, who also owned Connington and Leighton Bromswold, as well as estates in Northamptonshire and Lincolnshire. The Red Book of Thorney records that after the Norman Conquest, Turkill left his lands and returned to his Danish kinsmen. His Sawtry lands were then given by William the Conqueror to Earl Waltheof who had married the King's niece Judith. William had already granted to her several large areas of forests and lands in Northamptonshire, including 500 acres at Fotheringhay. Earl Waltheof appears to have been an over-ambitious and greedy man who did not enjoy the King's favour for too long. He was executed in 1075 and his lands at Sawtry were held by his widow Judith, certainly until the Domesday Book was compiled.

Waltheof's beheaded body makes a brief appearance in a later chapter when I refer to a legend about him at Croyland Abbey. But that must wait . . .

Judith's daughter, Maud, married Simon de St Lys (who built Fotheringhay Castle), and their son, another Simon, founded the abbey at Sawtry in 1147.

And all that to explain, briefly, how Monks' Wood came into the possession of the Abbey, whose land it remained until the Dissolution in 1536. It then passed into private ownership again until it was finally purchased by the Nature Conservancy in 1953. It is now being managed to restore its former character and to provide favourable conditions for its plant and animal life. The reserve is used extensively for research and a permit must be obtained from the warden before entering.

* * *

I stand for a few moments and lean on the gate, looking over into the density of trees that hold so much history. You can feel the concentrated warmth of the breath of ages being exhaled from the wood. The shaded rides and the damp undergrowth have a way of protecting not only the rare insects and flowers, but also the ghosts of all those who have ever been here.

I leave Monks' Wood and pass under the railway bridge of the main line, where trains now speed at well over 100 m.p.h., and enter the quiet village of Woodwalton. The chestnut trees welcome you with a calm drowsiness that seems to say " what's all the fuss about?" The village always looks attractive with its cottages and pub, and the same senior citizens always appear to be sitting in the same position on the same village seat. They stare at me and wonder again why I am passing through their day, showing such interest or curiosity.

The road rises to cross a ridgeway, where some more modern excavations are taking place and, on the crest of the rise, I stop to appreciate the truly impressive view there is over the fens. In the far distance the brickyard chimneys, from Fletton to Whittlesey, stretch along the horizon like branchless trunks of a petrified forest.

From this vantage point you would not think you were about to enter the traditionally bleak fens—and very few are as bad as some critics would have you believe. To be sure I've chosen a good day and a good approach. From Woodwalton the narrow road dips down between harlequin fields of yellow rape and jade-green wheat. In the middle distance is an attractive row of Lombardy poplars—which, for once, enhance a fenland scene. A warm breeze rises from the valley, rich with good husbandry. In one field the chequered cattle graze contentedly, as if it's the only thing in the world they have to do; waiting, perhaps, for the monks to call them in for milking. The passive wind flows through a sea of barley like a swiftly returning tide. The pattern of light hypnotizes. A kestrel hovers overhead like a high hang-glider teasing the air. A jay flashes from a nearby tree and disappears over the hill.

Looking into the smoky-blue distance I take a deep breath and feel excited at the thought of spending another summer exploring a landscape I love so much—and at the same time, realize how lucky I am in being paid for something I get great pleasure out of doing in the first place.

I know that as I make my way down through Great Raveley and Upwood to Woodwalton Fen I am preparing myself for a very special experience—not only a returning to a favourite remnant of the Great Fen itself, but a returning to a place potent with memories.

The 514 acres of Woodwalton Fen form one of the last fragments of the great tracts of unreclaimed vegetation which occupied this part of the fenland basin until the drainage operations of the seventeenth century changed the rest of our landscape for ever.

Woodwalton contains reed and mixed vegetation, rough grassland and extensive areas of sallow carr. Work is always being done to reduce the amount of scrub and carr so that the growth of reed and other vegetation is encouraged. All this is being achieved with considerable success but it's only half the story. In a few moments I shall be talking with the warden, Gordon Mason, and he will make the fen a " living world ", not a text-book quotation.

The fen (or reserve as it's now called) has been well known for decades, especially among botanists and entomologists, because it has provided the only habitat in Britain for some species of fen plant and insects—particularly the fen violet and the large copper butterfly.

I turn down the narrow path that leads to the fen, call at Mr Mason's house to let him know I'm around, arrange with his wife to have a chat with him later, and then persuade my travel-battered car to hobble down the very rough track to the bridge, where I can leave it, and forget it for a couple of hours.

When I step on to the fen I hold my breath again at the immediate silence; not silence, but stillness. The silence I realize is broken by the trilling and gossip of birds, by the crisp rustling of reeds and the trembling of leaves. But there is stillness. The stillness of an ancient, unspoilt world which, for me, has a very real, individual spirit of its own.

You cannot be indifferent to it. The atmosphere changes immediately no, that's not true, the atmosphere does not change, you do. Footsteps are suddenly absorbed by the soft, black peat soil. The modern world is something you have suddenly left behind, locked outside on that other side of the bridge. This is no ordinary nature reserve. This is something we shall probably never see again—a world of nature that has been cared for by a man in love with nature, *and* by his father before him; seventy or eighty years of dedication, experience and expert knowledge.

" This fen," I remember Gordon Mason saying to me, " has been more than my work, it's been my garden and my hobby, seven days a week, all my life. I feel as if I was meant to do this. It's been my life. I've been very lucky."

I know that when I talk with Gordon Mason later in this chapter he will be passing on to me words of wisdom, for his life on this fen has made him a quiet and wise man, a man who has listened, felt and watched, alone.

So, there is the stillness, and there are the smells. The timely awareness that the air here is always sweet with the scent of earth, water, reeds, weeds, grass and wild flowers—meadow-sweet, lady's-smock, white campion, hemp agrimony, wild rose, yellow flag, and even the nettles.

Along the first ride there are silver birch trees, oak, beech, willow and aspen. Insects jump from plant to plant and the brown water is as dark and secret as a mystery.

I go first to an old lodge known as ' The Bungalow '— originally a shooting lodge for the Honourable Charles Roths-child, to whom the reserve owes its survival and, through whose generosity, the fen was made available to the Society for the Promotion of Nature Reserves in 1919. In 1954 the Society leased the reserve to the Nature Conservancy.

I first came to this fen with a group of eleven-year-old schoolchildren and, although I have been to it several times since, I can never approach the clearing round ' The Bungalow ' now without hearing their bright laughter and persistent questions. We had recently been on a schools visit to Belgium and this was to be the last chance we would all have of being together before the summer holidays—and before they all went their separate ways. The battlefields of Waterloo and the lace-makers of Bruges were now a long way away as we sat there on the thick grass, near that " house on stilts " on a piece of ancient England. But it was there where we were able to share again some of the work we'd done in a foreign land, the writing and tape-recording of a week that had its own history. The sun was hot. We'd brought a picnic. And the girls (as a special privilege) danced to a tune that had haunted our week away from the fens. The trees and reeds listened and, one felt, understood the paradox of something so passing and yet so permanent. That scene and that summer are gone, but something remains.

Certainly, I can never approach that clearing now without hearing echoes of their laughter, without seeing again the graceful dancing of those bare-footed girls, or without hearing that music. That piece of grass always was, and still is, greener than anywhere else in the fens. There is an enchanting, hypnotic atmosphere about the spot that keeps me there for most of the afternoon. The trees, reeds, weeds and wild flowers all *look* the same; the birds are still making the same sounds; but the children are missing. The people who shared that day are no longer there. And there is an eerie emptiness as well as a stillness. Nothing of that particular summer can of itself return, and yet it is worth coming back to listen to the echoes, to watch the shadows, and to remember.

And this fen is big enough in many ways to hold many memories and many experiences. Walk down any of the rides and you enter a world of such tranquillity that life is immediately enriched, the value of living increased.

The man who has cared for this fen with such devotion for many years is the person to take up the story now. Gordon

Mason is, as I've already said, a quiet man, a gentle man, approaching retirement with some understandable fear, and a man who has gained specialized knowledge of· nature conservancy at first hand. His ' university ' has been Woodwalton Fen. His experience is sought after by people from Sussex to Loch Lomond. The experts come to him.

He was born within a hundred yards of where he now lives. Apart from his war service he has spent his life in this lonely corner of the fen country. His father was the warden (or keeper, as they were called then) before him and he can remember being carried round the fen as a child on his father's shoulders.

" It was my world. It was all I knew. I didn't want anything else."

" How old were you when you realized that you wanted to take over from your father and do the same kind of work?"

" Oh, I think I always knew that I was being prepared for it, and I certainly wanted to continue what he was trying to do. Working with nature gives you something to live for."

That statement makes me reach for my pen and I look closely again at the man to whom such phrases come as natural as breath. His intense blue eyes have the sharpness of a man who has trained his sight to take in a universe at a glance.

" It's true, the moment I step on to that fen I know if there's a reed out of place."

And I believe him. He knows every plant and insect there is. A caterpillar crawls on to his hand and he tells me what sort of moth it will become. He watches the complete cycle of nature year after year, from the egg to the egg and the seed to the seed.

" We counted two hundred different species of moth in one night on this fen . . . we might have found more."

At this moment I am taken to see one of the rarest sights in Britain—a large copper butterfly, a beautiful, deep orange, silk-like insect that can only be found on this fen. And how this butterfly survives in Woodwalton at all is a saga in itself. Would you believe that rare butterflies depend, to some extent, on cows? Gordon Mason explains:

" The balance of nature is very delicate indeed. Sometimes I wonder if even the scientists realize how delicate it is . . . The large copper, for instance, relies on the greatwater-dock for its food supply and, over the years, I've discovered that cattle are the best way of propagating greatwater-dock. They ' poach ' the ground and create natural seed-pots for the greatwater-dock to grow in. It can be done artificially, of course, but the cattle are all part of my plan for making this fen a natural success . . . You can't hurry nature . . . you have to learn how to be patient . . . it can take years to discover how to increase one plant, or insect."

" How many cattle do you have on the fen now?"

" About forty Galloways."

" Why Galloways?"

" Because they're hardy and can stand a severe winter. And they make good beef. You mustn't forget that the cattle are also intended for the market. They earn money for us."

" This is a fairly recent innovation, is it?"

" Well, let's put it this way, we've reintroduced cattle on to the fen in recent years but there is a tradition of them. In the old days, in Lord Rothschild's time and before, parts of the fen were used as holdings for cattle on their way from Scotland to London."

" You spoke about the balance of nature; what other examples have you?"

" Well so much of nature depends on other parts of nature that I think it's dangerous for man to decide what it is *he* wants to get rid of—for instance, I remember once being asked to clear the fen of a certain species of grass and yet I knew that within the stalk of that grass was the only place where a certain species of moth would lay its eggs. Destroy the grass and you destroy the moth . . . A few years ago I noticed that there were not many toads or frogs on the fen and so the number of snakes declined too. When the toads returned, the snakes returned. Everything has its place in nature and I believe it's important that we should know what we're doing. And you can only know from *experience*. Experience takes a long time too!"

There are many other subjects that Gordon Mason talks about because he is a man who has gained a tremendous insight into the natural world from his work on Woodwalton Fen. He talks of the ' mosaic of open and mixed fen ', of the ' glades ' and the ' rides ', of the need to watch and be patient, of the importance of the ' little things '.

We stand looking out over this lovely countryside and feel

the warmth of the day. I ask Gordon if there is any special moment he cherishes in his memory from his life on the fen.

"They're all special moments. Each day has something."

"What time of the day do you most like being on the fen? In the morning?"

"In the evening; the best time for me is a spring evening between six and half-past. It becomes so very still then, so very quiet. It's beautiful. I love quietness and a spring evening on this fen is perfect peace."

I hope when the day comes Gordon will have a happy and contented retirement. He deserves it for he has given much to protect a very rare and special world. We owe him, and his kind, a lasting gratitude. I hope the Woodwalton nightingales will sing for him wherever he is and maybe a large copper butterfly will one day bless his smaller garden. His devotion to Woodwalton Fen will not, I trust, go unsung for it would not have been the same without him, or his father. When he goes something of the fen will go too, and its spirit will change; it's bound to. But let us hope that his example will not be forgotten or ignored.

"Working with Nature gives you something to live for."

I shall remember this day for a long time.

* * *

Driving home through such efficiently farmed countryside I realize that the beauty of this land comes from well-ordered cultivation. The wilderness can be beautiful in its own raw and haphazard way; wild mountains and forests can be beautiful in their ancient majesty that owes little to man. But a land that has been carefully cared for and preserved, that has been tamed and worked, that exists because of a long tradition of husbandry—such a land has a beauty of its own, orderly, civilized, at harmony with men's labours and the elements.

Looking over the immaculate fields of carrots, celery, potatoes, wheat and sugar beet in this lovely evening light, it becomes the land's turn to ask "What am I without you?", for it could not achieve such beauty of itself. But the men who are responsible for this land have already gone home, their work for the day is over and the trees are silent.

2

A *"Piece of Purple Pomp"*

Before taking myself off again into the fens I am going to digress westwards to a place that has several distinct connections with the fen country. It is a place that has every right to be part of this book, both because of its history and also because it is one of the most famous places on the banks of the River Nene.

It is, for me, also one of the most English scenes I know, especially in summer with its meadows, trees, cottages and cattle all looking specially arranged for a photograph or painting.

It is a place that has been, according to one antiquary, " distinguished beyond any other place in Britain (except the capital) by the aggravated misfortunes of Royalty ".

It is a place that has all the essence of the kind of English landscape I would like to remember if ever I become an exile; a place that appeals both from a distance and at close quarters; a place that always graces a summer and breathes an air of timelessness that is not destroyed by theories, or statistics, or loyalties.

That place, I will now reveal, is Fotheringhay, a quiet, stone village by the silent river, but always vibrant with the troubles and events of history—a history which is, I agree, distinguished by the number of eminent heads that have been severed from noble bodies.

I was persuaded to write of Fotheringhay in this chapter because a day of rain kept me indoors yesterday, and when I'm indoors, aching to get out, I tend to pace up and down my room in between long periods of staring out of my window. And it was through these precincts that Mary Queen of Scots was brought in July 1587 to be buried in the cathedral, until, in 1612, her son James I, had her body removed to Westminster

Abbey. What is particularly disturbing about the poor lady's burial in Peterborough is that she was actually beheaded in Fotheringhay on 8 February 1578, five months before the great funeral procession through this city. But we will return to that episode in a moment.

It is the thought of sharp, thudding blades on white, human necks that makes me pause for a while to ask why Fotheringhay has such an appeal, why such an air of peace, comfort, romance and tranquillity pervades the place in view of its bloody happenings. Indeed, if some of the accounts we have inherited from earlier historians are wholly true, then the happenings have not only been bloody but they have also been distinctly sinister.

One of the more macabre events associated with the place belongs to the eleventh century when William the Conqueror granted Fotheringhay to his niece Judith, mentioned in the previous chapter. Judith, you will remember, was married to Earl Waltheof who eventually lost his head for being rather greedy—a common enough penalty in those days, no doubt, but one made memorable by the fact that this particular subject's head continued praying aloud after it had parted company from the rest of his body.

My own feeling is that if you're going to pray in a crisis you should start soon enough.

Waltheof's head will appear again later, as promised, when it miraculously rejoins his body and becomes the cause of ecclesiastical controversy and pilgrimages to another part of the fen country.

The threads of history and legend are indeed intricately woven, and places which now have very little to do with each other have these small but fascinating connections in the past.

But, to get back for a moment to the posthumously praying Waltheof and his wife Judith: they had a daughter, called Maud, who inherited her father's estates and she married Simon de St Lys, who built Fotheringhay Castle in 1100 and also founded a nunnery. Their son, Simon de St Lys junior, was to continue the good work forty-seven years later by founding the abbey at Sawtry.

So, Fotheringhay, Sawtry, Croyland and Peterborough are inevitably woven into this story as their lands, families, princes and fortunes were frequently complicated and inseparable. But knowing a little of how interrelated they are you cannot look at one without considering the other.

When Maud's husband died she married David, King of Scotland, and so Fotheringhay's long association with royal families continued, including along the way the birth of Richard III, the death of Mary Stuart, and visits from Elizabeth I. Peterborough's other buried queen, Catherine of Aragon, might also have been a victim of Fotheringhay if Henry had had his way, but she refused to go and spent her last years at Kimbolton instead. What strange, haphazard, accidental and devious twists the course of history has taken! Who might have ruled us but for some snap decision, fit of temper or love-affair?

*   *   *

Before quoting from a contemporary and lurid description of Mary's execution it might be better to stroll round the village of today, if only to let the dust settle and the blood cool.

There are several approaches to Fotheringhay and you will find all of them attractive. The least impressive is, I think, the quiet road from Wansford, Yarwell and Nassington. Not uninteresting by any means but, as an approach to the village itself it lacks the majestic aspect that other roads offer. Somehow you are there before you realize you're there and you reach the church too soon. My favourite approach is along the road from Oundle and Tansor so that there is more time to take in the truly magnificent sight of the church on its rise, reflected in the calm waters of the Nene, its distinctive lantern tower crowned with its golden weather-vane, a falcon encircled by a fetterlock.

Cattle are grazing in the pastures. The smell of meadow flowers fills the air, and the composition of the scene is almost perfect. To the right of the narrow hump-backed bridge is the mound on which the castle stood. One boulder and a small hill are not much but you are suddenly transported back, in quite a theatrical way, to a very different age.

The countryside all round Fotheringhay has, for me, a special magic. Tansor, Cotterstock, Woodnewton, Glapthorn and Southwick are all villages of unusual charm with fine houses and good memories. I remember particularly evenings of poetry and music at Southwick Hall, with drifts of snow-drops in the spring and furnaces of leaves in the autumn.

I said a moment ago that my favourite approach to Fother-inghay is from Tansor, but I think my favourite view of the church is from the riverside at Elton, a village a mile or two to the east. Here the River Nene enjoys the last of its natural, winding journey through parklands, harvest fields and white willows, before entering the fens where it has, like other fenland rivers, been straightened out over the years by different generations of engineers trying to keep the fens from flooding.

I remember one evening in particular when I crossed the river by the lock and walked along the grassy path by the water. It was the perfection of all summer evenings. The bright red setting sun appeared to be caught like a hot-air balloon in a hedge at the end of a barley field. The sun's low, dying light made the reeds' feathers glow golden and heraldic. The first stars were already reflected in the darkening water and a frightened heron rose from the shadows. On the other side of the river the cattle stood silent and motionless. The trees were draped like green velvet curtains round a proscenium arch. And then, in the distance, I saw the royal church charcoaled on the skyline, its weather-vane dazzling, its history filling the air. I stood and watched until its silhouette was absorbed by the night, then I turned and walked slowly back to the village. By this time the moon was up. I did not see it first in the sky but caught instead in the flat green leaves on the river—a water-lily of rare beauty.

But I was going to tell you, before all these reminiscences crept in, about the death at Fotheringhay of the village's most famous prisoner. Or rather, I was going to leave it to that earlier chronicler, Froude, to describe it for you in his own convincing style, and I think it's time he took over.

> . . . she descended the great staircase to the great hall . . . at the upper end of the hall stood the scaffold, twelve feet square and two feet and a half high. It was covered with black cloth; a low rail ran round it covered with a black cloth also, and the Sheriff's guard of halberdiers were ranged on the floor below to keep off the crowds. On the scaffold was the block, black like the rest; a square black cushion was placed behind it, and, behind the cushion, a black chair . . . The axe leant against the rail, and two masked figures stood like mutes on either side at the back. The Queen of Scots, as

Peterborough Cathedral

The site of Sawtry Abbey

Boathouse built of fen reed, Woodwalton Fen

The 'Bungalow' or 'House on Stilts', Woodwalton Fen

View of the fens from Woodwalton village

Woodwalton Fen drove

Reeds on Woodwalton Fen

Deserted farmyard (now a new housing estate)

Fotheringhay church, on the River Nene

Pews and pulpit, Fotheringhay church

Skyscape near Huntingdon

Fishing the Great Ouse, near St Ives

she swept in, seemed as if coming to take part in some solemn pageant. Not a muscle of her face could be seen to quiver; she ascended the scaffold with absolute composure. [Then] on her knees she repeated the Psalm *"In te, Domine, confido"*. When the Psalm was finished she felt for the block and muttered *"In manus, Domine, tuas, commendo animan meam"*. The hard wood seemed to hurt her for she placed her hands under her neck. The executioner gently removed them lest they should deaden the blow, and then one of them, holding her slightly, the other raised the axe and struck. The scene had been too trying even for the practised headsman of the Tower. His aim wandered. The blow fell on the knot of the handkerchief and scarcely broke the skin. She neither moved nor spoke. He struck again, this time effectively. The head hung by a shred of skin, which he divided without withdrawing the axe; and at once a metamorphosis was witnessed, strange as was ever wrought by wand or fabled enchanter. The coif fell off and the false plaits. The laboured illusion vanished. The lady who had knelt before the block was in the maturity of grace and loveliness. The executioner, when he raised the head as usual to show it to the crowd, exposed the withered features of a grizzled, wrinkled old woman . . .

Well, that's part of it, and I can almost hear you saying " and *you* find this place beautiful and with an air of tranquillity; that *this* is the piece of England you would take with you into exile?" It does make you think, doesn't it? It makes you stop to ask if perhaps we grumble too much about the twentieth century. But then, the twentieth century hasn't been too sensitive about getting rid of people, in their millions. And Fotheringhay does have some special atmosphere about it that makes it different from many other English villages.

Walk round to the south side of the church, climb over the stone stile, sit by the river for a while in the midsummer sun, and you will feel what I mean. I think my photographer has caught it as much as any camera can—after all, you can't photograph ' feelings ' or ' vibrations in the air '.

Having looked at Fotheringhay from the riverside you can then wander along to ' The Falcon ' for some excellent refreshment before visiting the mound where once the castle stood and the above ghastly deed was performed.

It's not easy to forget that deed, for several reasons. And what do you do with a royal body that has had its head chopped off, a body deeply out of favour with the reigning monarch and her court? You see, Mary, beheaded on 8 February 1578, was not buried in Peterborough until 31 July of the same year. So what happened to the poor lady in the meantime?

There had been much indecision about Mary's trial, imprisonment and execution. She and Elizabeth were not only powerful, independent women but royal queens in their own rights. Despite the threats to her throne and all the intrigues between the two courts, Elizabeth was reluctant to put to death another queen. But the act was carried out under her seal and the body had to be buried. But where, and when? Until this decision was made Mary's corpse lay embalmed, wrapped in a wax winding sheet, placed in a lead coffin and remained locked in Fotheringhay Castle. The body's organs, including the heart, had already been taken out and given to the county sheriff who had them buried secretly somewhere in the castle. The rest of the Scottish queen was eventually taken to Peterborough on the last day of July 1587 for its twenty-five year interment before being moved yet again to Westminster. Was she even buried in Peterborough that day? In a moment we shall see. An irony she would not have smiled over was that she, a Catholic Queen, was given a Protestant burial service.

By the time she was finally granted a full Christian and State burial in Peterborough her body was " no longer lovely to look upon " and, in another romantic retelling of her story, we read that she was in fact buried secretly on the night before her official State funeral because

> " the weather being hot, they feared
> She would not hold the burying."

I'm quoting now from ' The Burial of a Queen ' from *Tales of the Mermaid Tavern* by the poet Alfred Noyes. We don't seem to get poetry books like that any more—over 200 pages of story-telling. Story-telling in verse-form is surely one of the oldest, most enchanting and effective, spell-casting, compelling forms of all. I would like to quote all of ' The Burial of a Queen ' but it is about a thousand lines long and so I can only give you a taste. I urge you to look up the whole of it for yourself some time to recapture something of that old tradition of telling stories in taverns long before juke-boxes and computerized bar-games.

In the poem, the story of Mary's burial is told by sexton

Timothy Scarlett, the now grey old nephew of Peterborough's
most celebrated sexton, old Robert Scarlett himself; the only
man known to have buried two queens in the same abbey.
Timothy Scarlett arrives at The Mermaid on All Souls' Eve.
The tavern is busy with its usual customers, including Ben
Jonson, John Ford, Michael Drayton, Thomas Lodge and
Drummond of Hawthornden—not a bad collection of authors
to have in for the evening. Robert Herrick, we hear, has gone
to dine with John Donne, and some of the other well-known
regulars are absent—Christopher Marlowe, John Lyly and
George Peele. Nevertheless, the grave-digging-weary Timothy
finds an eager audience around the fireside ready to hear about
the famous burial of 1587. After a long introduction we are told
about his distinguished uncle, of how he buried poor Catherine
of Aragon and later, with the help of the story-teller, Mary
Queen of Scots Herself.

The listeners refill their jugs and ask the narrator to
continue.

> . . . When you hear her name
> Your hearts will leap. Her beauty passed the bounds
> Of modesty men say, yet—she died young!
> We buried her at midnight. There were few
> That knew it; for the high State funeral
> Was held upon the morrow, Lammas Morn.
> Anon, you shall hear why. A strange thing that,
> To see the mourners weeping round a hearse
> That held a dummy coffin. Stranger still
> To see us lowering the true coffin down
> By torchlight, with some few of her true friends,
> In Peterborough Cathedral, all alone . . .

At that stage of the narrative I have to admit to being a bit
disillusioned myself. There was I, at the beginning of this
chapter, thinking about the great funeral procession making its
slow, dignified approach to the cathedral, only to learn that
the queen was buried in secret, at midnight, with hardly
anyone there. There was a procession, it is true, but . . . I'll let
Timothy Scarlett continue

> . . . my uncle lived
> A mile or more from Peterborough then,
> And, past his cottage, in the dead of night
> Her royal coach came creeping through the lanes,
> With scutcheons round it and no crowd to see,

> And heralds carrying torches in their hands,
> And none to admire, but him and me, and one—
> A pedlar-poet who lodged with us that week.

Timothy Scarlett rises from his bench, picks up his spade and leans upon it. " I've got to feel my spade " he says, as he begins to recite some of the pedlar-poet's verses.

> All in the middle of the night
> My face was at the pane;
> When, creeping out of his cottage-door
> To wait for the coach of a queen once more,
> Old Scarlett, in the moonlight
> Beckoned to me again.

> He stood beneath a lilac-spray,
> Like Father Time for dole,
> In Reading Tawny cloak and hood,
> With mattock and with spade he stood,
> And far away to southward
> A bell began to toll . . .

> They carried her down with singing,
> With singing sweet and low,
> Slowly round the curve they came,
> Twenty torches dropping flame,
> The heralds that were bringing her
> The way we all must go

> With torches and with scutcheons,
> Unhonoured and unseen,
> With the lilies of France in the wind astir,
> And the Lion of Scotland over her,
> Darkly, in the dead of night,
> They carried the Queen, the Queen . . .

And so, through that summer night the three men slowly went: Robert Scarlett, Timothy Scarlett, and the anonymous pedlar-poet, following the silent royal procession " through a world of innocence and sleep " until they reached Peterborough Cathedral. And there, by the light of a few torches, they began to bury the lady once honoured in France and Scotland. But here the story takes on another mystery. Old Scarlett's nephew continues:

> We laid her in her grave. We closed the tomb.
> With echoing footsteps all the funeral went;
> And I went last to close and lock the doors;
> Last, and half-frightened of the enormous gloom

That rolled along behind me as one by one
The torches vanished . . .
But, as I turned the key, a quivering hand
Was laid upon my arm. I turned and saw
That foreigner with the olive-coloured face.
From head to foot he shivered as with cold.
He drew me into the shadows of the porch.
" Come back with me " he whispered, and slid his hand,
Like ice it was, along my wrist and slipped
A ring upon my finger, muttering quick,
As in a burning fever, " All the wealth
Of Eldorado for one hour! Come back!
I must go back and see her face again!
I was not there, you see, the day she—died!
You'll help me with the coffin—Not a soul
Will know. Come back! One moment, only one!"
I thought the man was mad, and plucked my hand
Away from him. He caught me by the sleeve
And sank upon his knees, lifting his face
Most piteously to mine. " One moment! See!
I loved her!"
I saw the moonlight glisten on his tears,
Great, long, slow tears they were; and then, my God!
As his face lifted and his head sank back
Beseeching me—I saw a crimson thread
Circling his throat as though the headman's axe
Had cloven it with one blow, so shrewd, so keen,
The head had slipped not from the trunk. I gasped;
And, as he pleaded, stretching his head back,
The wound, O like a second awful mouth,
The wound began to gape. I tore my cloak
Out of his clutch. My keys fell with a clash.
I left them where they lay and with a shout
I dashed into the broad white empty road.
There was no soul in sight. Sweating with fear
I hastened home, not daring to look back;
But as I turned the corner I heard the clang
Of those great doors and knew he had entered in.

At this point of the story I imagine all who listened
swallowed, took a deep breath, called for another drink and
wondered what sort of corrupt face the poor demented lover
would have found severed from a corpse now five months old.
And what about the State funeral? Well, that, we are told by
Timothy Scarlett,

Was held on Lammas Day. A wondrous sight
For Peterborough! For myself I found
Small satisfaction in a catafalque
That carried a dummy coffin. Nonetheless,
The pedlar thought that as a Solemn Masque,
Or piece of Purple Pomp, the thing was good.

The masque, the host of mourners, the lords and ladies, all gathered at the Bishop's Palace, among them Monsieur du Preau, her French confessor; Sir George Savile; Sir Andrew Noel; two great bishops; sixteen Scottish and French noblemen and sword-bearers; and many followers. After the funeral service, " at which a mighty *Miserere* was sung for her soul ", the chief mourners returned to the Bishop's Palace " for a great feast worthy of their sorrow ", which cost over £100.

At the end of the day the sexton's nephew returned to lock the cathedral and there, once more, he found " the olive-coloured gentleman " at Mary's tomb. But this time the tomb was open.

And then, two shadows passed against the West,
Two blurs of black against the crimson stain,
Slowly, O very slowly, with bowed heads,
Leaning together, and vanished into the dark . . .

The story is by no means over and there are many other remarkable episodes in ' The Burial of a Queen ', including the significance of that ruby ring.

So, was all the purple pomp and ceremony for nothing, for no more than other pedlar-poets to dream about? Oh, I don't know; there was, after all, pageantry of some sort. I still like to imagine the occasion and am even tempted to put on a recording of the funeral music that Purcell wrote for another royal Mary, for it is noble and moving music for any sad event. But this part of her story ends here, in the middle of my summer. In 1612 James I had his mother's body—or shall we say coffin?—removed to Westminster Abbey, and we in Peterborough are left with our one queen, Catherine of Aragon, and, of course, Old Scarlett himself. There can be no doubt about him. What would he say about it all, I wonder?

Old Scarlett—
Robert Scarlett
to give him his full name—

deserves an entry in
the Guinness Book of Records
because, of all grave-diggers
who ever lived, he
had the distinction
of burying two queens
in the same abbey—
Katharine of Aragon
and Mary Queen of Scots,
two noble ladies who came
with purple pomp and ceremony
to share the same unlikely ground
at a place once called Medehamstede;
a city more famous today
for its diesel engines,
a struggling football team,
and some new houses which Old Scarlett
would have been ashamed to have built
even for the dead.

Now I shan't be at all surprised to hear that there are historical inaccuracies in the above narrative, but you must admit that it has all the ingredients of a good yarn to tell by a log fire in a cosy pub on a winter evening. They are quite compelling stories too for a summer's evening, as I've found out from reading them to friends in the shadowy bat-time of these cloistered twilights. The coffee has gone cold, the lager flat, and the sandwiches lie uneaten as these figures have returned to live their lives, loves and deaths for us.

They carried her down with singing,
With singing sweet and low,
Slowly round the curve they came
Twenty torches dropping flame,
The heralds that were bringing her
The way we all must go.

3
Going to St Ives . . .

Now we know that summer has really arrived for, as someone rightly observed in the Press the other day the country roads have just been given a liberal dressing of loose-chippings and the grass verges reek of tar.

I quite like the smell of tar myself but I do agree about the excess of loose-chippings. For the last few days nearly every road I've travelled has had its annual treatment. It's as regular as sheep-dipping or beating the bounds; as predictable as Easter Monday or rain for the first Test Match. But we must use roads, and so I press on through the barrage of machine-gun fire that attacks me from below. Surely they don't have enough loose-chippings to cover the whole country? Surely we shall escape, some time? Perhaps in the end, I have to admit, I am being ungrateful. If we need this annual advent of peppering the country roads with loose-chippings to guarantee the arrival of summer, then long live the tar and the loose-chippings yet, for the seductive warmth of today is something not to be missed.

And when I use that word ' warmth ' I do so almost with affection. It isn't just another degree of heat, not just another description of the climate. It is a state of being—like a warm personality, or a warm colour. The kind of warmth that does something to you, that makes you feel better.

Today is a day of such perfect warmth that you cannot be (or rather do not *want* to be) positive about anything. You just want to bask in it like a contented dolphin in the July sea, or like a carefree cow in a summer meadow near Fotheringhay. Or, to remain human, you might want to do nothing more than sit in a deck-chair in the garden, listening to that poet of cricket commentators, John Arlott, whose unmistakable voice has droned through so many summers, spicing the air with his unique blend of information and imagery.

All around me today is a scene to make such idyllic laziness possible. You can exist on a day like this with a clear conscience in a world where the activities of man no longer really matter. It is a day for sun and white clouds. A *sky* day when the earth is only the stage on which some other drama might take place. The clouds are the actors playing their Falstaffian roles with slow dignity. The stage is important of course and I'm prepared to claim that in this part of England we have the best stage in the country for the sky's latest performance.

When I take my eyes away from the clouds for a moment and look at the earth I have to give it a round of applause too. The green, leathery leaves of the sugar-beet soak up the sun. The potatoes are delicately dressed in their pink flowers and give not a thought to the day when they will become chips, or frozen, or mashed. The grey ears of wheat stand still and slender, low rows of firework-sparklers waiting to be lit. The poppies are already alight, bright red flames dazzling the day. The silk sheen of the barley gently shows which way the wind is blowing, and the distant woods jealously hold their cool darkness like a secret. Mallow and ragwort, cornflower and daisy, decorate the grass verges. Skylarks sing, ecstatically, of course, as if they too are grateful for such a day and are trying equally hard to say so. I watch them hovering, trembling moth-like, their quivering wings concentrating on their intense song until, after several minutes, they fall slowly, like floating ash-keys, back to earth.

An occasional car passes, its driver wondering what an idle fellow like me is doing leaning on a gate in the country, staring into the sky, scribbling something into a note-book and then looking blithely pleased with himself.

On a day like this I have to wonder how anyone can fail to find this part of the country beautiful. I know I'm a bit chauvinistic about it but the great, rich, lonely and uncluttered spaces have so much to offer that I cannot understand why so many people find them dull and uninteresting. Perhaps I ought to be grateful. Today the variety of colour is so generous that even to eyes that have looked so often before there is a new excitement.

I have travelled over the fens through Upwood, Great Raveley, Wistow, Bury and Warboys on my way to St Ives.

There are remarkable vistas over Wistow Fen, Turf Fen and especially Pidley-cum-Fenton Fen where you look down from a height over an enormous plain that stretches away to Chatteris and Sutton in the Isle. On a good day they say you can see Ely Cathedral twenty miles away, but I think you would need to have very good eyes or be in an air-balloon.

The temptation is to go towards that horizon, but there will be other days for Ely and I keep to my plan, or intuition, and drive on into St Ives where, more than once, I have been able to pick up a bargain in a second-hand bookshop, or an equally good buy in some other shop, especially one near the bridge.

St Ives, like many another ancient town, can be a motorist's nightmare because of so many other motorists, vans and lorries; and, with the frustration, there can be an urgency to get through the town as quickly as possible if you are a bit short of patience. But this would be a great pity because, as I hope to explain in a moment, you are travelling through a town of unusual origin and I have always found its people and tradesmen most affable, even under the stern, watchful eye of Oliver Cromwell's statue.

If you are by any chance interested in a drop of really good Scotch, then it's worth visiting St Ives for one shop alone, the shop near the bridge I have just referred to, where you can gloat covetously over one hundred single-malt whiskies, some thirty-eight and fifty years old, with names to stir the imagination of anyone—including the Protector, perhaps! Your eyes follow slowly along the dim shelves, each bottle a mystery, holding the secrets of some remote glen and pride of an ancient clan. The guttural echoes and conspiracies of a different world are not very far away. The haunting phrases of old songs and the narrative of strange tales from the past lurk there. And *that's* with just looking at the labels! The darkness and the dust of the surroundings add to the sense of wonder and rareness of such a collection. Long may it reign. Long may such a shop remain at the foot of an ancient bridge by an ancient river. I was told that the Scots themselves have been known to come down to this part of England to reclaim some of their exported rarities. Are they genuine collectors, devotees, or bounty hunters? Or are they spies preparing for a massive invasion? Beware the sound of the pipes in St Ives, even on Burns' Night.

Some of the other shops I like to visit have gone, either

through fires or bulldozer. St Ives has suffered a lot from fires and the little second-hand bookshop (where I once picked up several first editions of Laurie Lee for a shilling each) was one of its latest victims.

There have been other changes too, some more deliberate, some well intentioned, and the town may have lost a lot of its original character. But there is still something about the history of St Ives which I think is worth relating here because it does have an influence on your feelings about the place when you explore it today.

It began as a riverside settlement in Anglo-Saxon times and was known then as Slepe—a slipway to a ford. As the position of its parish church suggests, the orginal community was well west of the present town centre. Its name was changed to St Ives after the discovery of the remains of Bishop Ivo—an early Christian believed to be of Persian origin who had come to preach in East Anglia and who then died at Slepe. His remains had healing powers (as so often happened with such pious relics—St Oswald of Peterborough and St Etheldreda at Ely, for instance) and were transferred to Ramsey Abbey in 970. In fact not only the remains of St Ivo but the village of Slepe itself became the possession of the new Benedictine abbey on the edge of the great undrained fens. Little wonder that with all its quickly acquired wealth and possessions it became known as " Ramsey the rich of gold and fee ". Its influence on places like St Ives was to last for a long time.

In 1107 a wooden bridge was built over the local stretch of the River Ouse and traders began arriving to sell and exchange their wares. In 1110 Henry I granted the monks of Ramsey an annual fair, to be held for a week from Easter Monday, " near the village of St Ivo de Slepe ". The fair became so popular that in the end it was decided that the stalls should become permanent buildings; and so began the town of St Ives as we know it today, a town that has grown up between its two main influences—the church and the river.

The Easter Fair was one of the most important and spectacular events in the country during the thirteenth and fourteenth centuries. Traders came, not only from all over England, but from the continent as well. Wool, wine, cloth and canvas; fruit, trinkets, jewels and spices, all were arranged to tempt the hundreds of people who travelled specially to St Ives.

Merchants from Flanders and northern France, from Italy and
Germany, from Spain and Egypt, all brought their wares,
accents and personalities to this most cosmopolitan of gatherings. In these days of world trade fairs, the European Community and international hypermarkets, we tend to think of
our native ancestors as a rather parochial lot, but they must
have enjoyed themselves enormously. Beer, pies and bread
were sold from barges on the river; bears and acrobats
performed in the streets; musicians played day and night. And
there were other entertainments too. One of the most common
complaints for disorderliness was against brothel keepers and
their prostitutes. One popular young lady who came to St Ives
and was always in great demand was known by her customers
as "sweet Dulcie from Oxford", and in 1300 a Mr Ralph
Clerk was accused of letting six of his houses to be used as
brothels when they should have been let to house more
respectable tenants. Prostitution, it seems, was quite big
business in such a small town where visitors' every need was
catered for. There is also an account of a certain carrier being
fined for allowing his overloaded cart to knock off three tiles
from the roof of a house which, to his disgrace, belonged to the
Abbot of Ramsey, no less. The carrier was severely reprimanded
and fined threepence for damage to the property. And all that
in days long before overloaded juggernauts came to dislodge a
few tiles, lamp-posts and houses in the twentieth century. I get
the feeling that you only need to stand on the market-place to
catch a scent of all that throbbing, down-to-earth life of 600
years back.

St Ives was proving such a popular trading place then that
by the end of the thirteenth century the now famous Monday
Market had been established as an important event in the
country. It continued to grow in reputation and prosperity,
outlasting, in the end, the importance of the Easter Fair which,
in many ways, was a victim of the Black Death.

By the early fifteenth century St Ives found that it needed a
new bridge. Why? Because the increasing weight of traffic
meant that the old one was no longer safe. Well, it's a familiar
story, and St Ives was pushing its luck a bit. After all, the old
timber bridge had only been there 300 years. Some towns have
had to wait much longer. Anyway, the townspeople won and
in 1414 the Abbot of Ramsey, believing also in the importance

of good communications and trade, agreed to build a new stone bridge over the river, using the Barnack stone which, as we have already seen, was in such demand then for the construction of ecclesiastical buildings.

It's an impressive bridge by any standard, with six arches and its almost unique chapel halfway across—there being, I believe, only two other such bridge chapels left in England.

The riverside walk, and that lovely view over the meadows, is surely one of the most attractive riverside scenes you could witness anywhere in the country, certainly in East Anglia. The water is broad and calm with the reflection of boats. The trees and fields, the cattle and distant church spire, all make it a rural picture of such charm that you have to believe in all the boasts about the supremacy of English landscape for a while.

The Great Ouse is a noble river and it passes through many lovely places. I shall be spending some time on it in a week or two when some friends take me out in their boat—but more of that later. I'm a bit vague on nautical terms at the moment and may, metaphorically, fall overboard before I embark.

Between the new bridge being built in the fifteenth century and today there were, of course, many other events and important changes in the life of St Ives. The reign of Henry VIII brought about differences in land ownership as well as religion, and the imposing statue of Oliver Cromwell in the Market Place is an unavoidable reminder of that character's association with the town. I suppose Cromwell must have been the most travelled man in England for his visits crop up everywhere you go. Charles Dickens is another ' famous person ' who seems to have been around quite a bit, unconsciously bestowing on towns, inns and shops the right to put up a plaque ' Dickens Was Here . . .'

Well, Cromwell was in St Ives and, although I shall be allowing him more space when I go to Huntingdon, he must have his mention in St Ives. The Lord Protector, always an opportunist, did move to the town to take possession of some new lands he had acquired and he did live in the parish for five years. Then the death of an uncle gave him an even greater increase in property and wealth, which meant moving to Ely. During the Civil War St Ives, like Huntingdon, Cambridge, and indeed much of the fens, were to become important places within the parliamentary zone.

St Ives, then, has had a good share of the fun, feasting, fighting, fairs and history that has gone on in this part of England. To rush through, or to ignore it, is to lose a real tang of the past; and the past isn't just a slice of life you can cut off and dispense with or deposit in the text-books. We are a product of the past. We will become the past, just as the future will become the present. History is a continual river into which we feed our own ripples, pollution and sunlight. When we wake up in the morning today will already be part of history. Trace the days back one by one and the people of four or five hundred years ago come laughing, bustling, shouting down the street. We, the present, are only the link between what has gone and what is to come. How strong, or important, our time will be is difficult to say, but one thing is sure, it is part of the chain or stream and we cannot, as far as I know, opt out without destroying the lot.

Yes, today is different—everywhere. But beneath the stones are a good many memories, traditions, families, beliefs and hopes. A town may grow, a population may multiply, but you cannot detach yourself from what has been if you wish to live. Our turn will come. In five hundred, or a thousand, years, what will the travellers and historians be saying of us? Much the same, I suppose. " They built bridges, had wars, held fairs, argued about religion, race, prostitution, went hungry, fed well, knocked people's houses down, made laws, served dictators, married, procreated, died."

I hope the fun and the fairs do not die out or change. We need the roundabouts and coconut shies to stop us taking ourselves too seriously. In many ways St Ives is like Brueghel's paintings come to life. You become involved in whatever might be happening.

*   *   *

If this town isn't enough for one day, then there are still plenty of interesting places within a few minutes' driving distance, camera-tempting villages that will take you away from the bustle of commerce—Hemingford Grey, Hemingford Abbots, Houghton, Bluntisham and Earith. Indeed a visit to Earith is an essential part of the day if you wish to appreciate fully just how great man's achievement has been in making the

Cambridgeshire fen country the richest, most fertile area of Britain. It may not be the photographer's paradise, as the Hemingfords are, but here you will see something of that dramatic story of fen drainage laid out before you in a way more vivid than any book can manage.

But let Earith wait for a moment and turn your attention to those tucked-away villages nearer to St Ives—Hemingford Grey and Hemingford Abbots. Between them they offer a good variety of interests with their two churches, a watermill, timber-framed cottages, a manor house, mellow stone buildings, rich gardens and trees. The riverside walks are specially attractive, but a view of the village from the river is even better. I shall be seeing these villages again, from ' the boat ', in a later chapter, but their charm is worth mentioning more than once.

As you approach Earith it is necessary also to take your mind back to the early seventeenth century and the year 1630, for it was here that the young Dutchman, Cornelius Vermuyden, began his ambitious draining operations when it was decided that these fens should, after all, be drained. In fact you may want to go even farther back to have an explanation of The Hermitage Lock which dominates this meeting-point of roads, rivers and fields. Before the fens were drained there was a raised causeway from Earith into the Isle of Ely and, in 1490, there is a reference to a J. Thompson who lived on the Earith Causeway and whose occupation was given as ' hermit '. Later there was a house built on the same site and called Hermitage House. When this was pulled down in 1939 a fifteenth-century stone cellar was discovered in the foundations and believed to be the home of the hermit. The name has been perpetuated in the new Hermitage Lock on the River Ouse.

But let us get back to 1631 and Vermuyden. Cornelius Vermuyden was only twenty-six when he came to this country in 1621. As an engineer he was unrivalled. He was invited to drain the Thames Marches near Dagenham, then the Great Park at Windsor and eventually the Royal Chase at Hatfield in Yorkshire.

Despite all the troubles he had with his labour force and the racial problems between the Yorkshire families and the Dutch workers he'd been forced to import, Vermuyden completed his tasks, much to the pleasure of the King. By his skill,

determination and personality he had overcome enormous
difficulties. He had succeeded against nature. He had succeeded
in a foreign land. He had won favour with the King. And he
was rich. On 6 January 1629 he received a knighthood and so,
at the age of thirty-four, became Sir Cornelius Vermuyden.

His celebrations were, perhaps, a little premature, for his
troubles in Yorkshire were by no means over and his troubles
in the fens had not yet begun. He was frequently engaged in
legal battles and land quarrels; he did not fully understand the
English temperament, and often met with contempt. His four
years' work at Hatfield were destroyed and his compatriots
were burned out of their homes and driven from the county.

It is not surprising therefore that his appointment in 1630, as
the engineer to the Gentlemen Adventurers' scheme to drain
the fens, was unpopular. Once again, finding the labour was a
problem. Local men were not only not interested in the work
but were also hostile to the whole idea of their country being
drained in the first place. It was a threat to their wildfowling,
shooting, fishing and reed-beds, to a way of life that had been
theirs for generations. The fen-tigers and the stiltmen, the
osiers and wildfowlers, wanted no interference from a foreigner
who only wanted to please a king.

But when Vermuyden had been set a task he was determined
to carry it out, even though, in the end, he had to rely on a
labour-force made up of prisoners of war. He decided his first
major problem was to straighten out the Great Ouse to get the
upland water more swiftly and safely to the Wash. To do this
he cut a new drain from Earith to Denver, twenty-one miles
long and as straight as a plumb-line. By taming the river at this
point he hoped to eventually succeed in draining the fens. It
was only a partial success and Vermuyden was to work on the
fens for the next twenty years, cutting new channels, building
dykes and sluices.

Vermuyden will also appear again in this account of summer
because I hope to spend a day on the Welney Marshes, that
wild tract of washland between the two cuts Vermuyden made
from Earith to Denver—known as the Old Bedford and the
New Bedford rivers after the Earls of Bedford who were the
chief backers for the project.

When you drive along roads in the fens that are above field-
level you are looking at fields which themselves are mostly

below sea-level. You will also notice that the river levels are frequently several feet above your own level, so the problem of keeping the fens drained can be clearly seen.

Vermuyden did not begin or complete the draining of the fens, but he was a major part of it and did as much as anyone to change the pattern of these lowlands. He died a lonely and relatively poor man in London in 1677, but Earith and the fens keep his name very much alive. Others carried on, and still do, to make this highly productive county a vital part of the English agricultural life.

Drive deeper into the fens from Earith, to Chatteris, Littleport, Welney or Wisbech, and you will see what I mean. It may not be acceptable in winter to those reared on more romantic scenes, but in summer with towering white clouds, a warm breeze, and the crops glowing, I do not see how it can fail to impress.

* * *

Throughout the summer the earth has slowly been changing colour. The sage-greens, jade-greens, smoky-greens and bottle-greens have become straw-yellow and golden. Each day of sun now makes a difference as we approach harvest. The barley is bleached and brittle. The wheat is growing heavy and walnut-brown. The potato foliage dries and shrivels after spraying. Soon the mechanical diggers will arrive and the air will be sweet with that satisfying smell of newly dug potatoes. Fruit ripens. The fields and men prepare.

But it is not only on farms that the summer's progress is recorded. On allotments and in back-gardens men gather the rewards of their earlier labours. The backaches from winter digging are forgotten as the arms carry home bunches of carrots, onions, beetroot, and baskets of peas, runner-beans and courgettes. Everywhere, at some time of the day or evening, someone can be seen taking from the earth what they and the earth have given. Their seeds multiplied and their work blessed.

4
When Huntingdon Was

" Huntingdonshire ", a popular guide was once able to say, " is a shy, demure county which likes to be left alone. A place of squires and yeomen . . . "

Ah, once! I suppose nearly every chapter in this book could start " once upon a time ". But Huntingdonshire, alas, is now officially extinct; a county no longer on the map; part of an older England gone for ever; drowned by the hungry floods of bureaucracy; simply wiped out and forgotten; forfeited to new administrations, new county halls, boundaries and councillors.

There may still be squires and yeomen left, owning and working the same farms; in fact I know there are and they still talk of their land as being " Huntingdonshire land ". And there was a time when this " shy, demure " part of the enlarged Cambridgeshire was an independent and ancient county in its own right, whose people like to be left alone to get on with their own rural way of life. They didn't get their own way in the end of course; life isn't like that any more. Their county had to go, and its evocative name had to go too; and everyone is now more or less resigned to his or her loss. It's not quite as bad as losing the Ridings of Yorkshire; that does seem to be an unnecessary piece of vandalism both to our geography and language; change for the sake of change, the abandoning of a lovely old word that, surely, for lovers of the English countryside and literature, meant much more than just a third of that rich county. I hope no one is cooking up ideas for doing away with the word ' shires ' and dividing us into ' states '. But we shouldn't be surprised at anything these days I suppose, and it might happen.

Taking identity and status away from a place does something to it by degrees, gives it an anonymous, don't-ask-me kind of look. Who will ask in a hundred years' time about Huntingdonshire, or Rutland, or the Soke of Peterborough, or the North Riding?

The populations of our counties are, admittedly, more shifting and cosmopolitan, and taking pride in one's native soil may seem a bit quaint. Transport has also done a lot to change the life and spirit of a place. We can now get out of our parishes much more easily to find the jobs with bigger pay-packets, better opportunities and more prestige. If we live near a main-line railway station and within a hundred miles of London, then the capital is an obvious attraction. And, of course, it works the other way. The provinces, the countryside, the relatively cheaper houses, are also more accessible. The dense concentration of life in the south is partly eased in the evenings when, like thousands of starlings flocking home to roost after their sunset ritual, the commuters crowd into King's Cross, Euston and Liverpool Street for the big migration north, to Huntingdon, Peterborough, Northampton, Cambridge, Norwich and all the surrounding villages that those stopping-places serve.

* * *

I may return to the Huntingdon of today later in this chapter but, for the moment, I want to look at those days when Huntingdon was the capital of its own shire and stage-coaches arrived at speeds slightly less than those of the 120 miles an hour Inter-City trains of today.

As early as the tenth century Huntingdon was important enough to have its own mint as well as market. At one time it had sixteen churches, three hospitals, and was considered by the Augustinian Canons to be the ideal place in which to build their first English priory. The town lost some of its importance after the Dissolution but regained ground—for different reasons—during the time of the Civil War when it became the headquarters of Oliver Cromwell and King Charles in turn. More prosperous times came with the stage-coach trade and many famous travellers were to break their journeys at the town's hostelries.

Some of those coaching inns are still there in one form or another and The George certainly retains something of its original character. Two sides of its seventeenth-century court-yard and open gallery remain, and, when outdoor productions of Shakespeare have been staged there, the place readily belongs to another age. The Falcon also survives and was used for a time as the Parliamentary headquarters by Cromwell. Although this gentleman has a habit of cropping up almost everywhere in England, Huntingdon can claim as much of him as most, for it was the town of his birth and the house where he was born is quite near the centre of town. A little nearer the shops are the remains of the old grammar school where he (like Samuel Pepys) was once a pupil. The building now houses the Cromwell Museum—a collection of portraits, documents, swords, gloves, hats and sundry belongings, all looking rather dull and unromantic.

Of much greater interest to me is Cowper House where the moody, romantic, gentle, mad, hymn-writing poet lived and fell in love with someone else's wife.

It was of this house that the Northamptonshire poet, John Clare, was to write when he passed through Huntingdon on his first visit to London and his own brief period of fame.

> When we passed through Huntingdon Mr. Gilchrist shewed me the house at the end of the town where Oliver Cromwell was born and the parsonage with its melancholy-looking garden at the other where Cowper had lived, which was by far the most interesting remembrance to me.

William Cowper was born in 1731 at Berkhamsted and enjoyed a protected and happy childhood until he was six years old. Then his mother died—a tragedy which was to over-shadow the rest of his life—and he was sent away to school. There he had the misfortune to become the lackey of an older, insensitive bully, who, as Cowper himself wrote later, he knew only by the buckles of his shoes. Even at that age he contemplated suicide, an ' escape route ' that he was to consider several times in his life. Eventually his father agreed to move him to Westminster School where he was at last able to settle down to the learning he so much wanted. While still in his teens he went to study law with a Mr Chapman of Ely Place and, at the age of nineteen, took up residence at the Middle Temple.

It was there, out of his intense loneliness and despair, that he discovered the power of poetry through the work of that other gentle but positive poet, George Herbert, a man of noble birth and humble nature, a man who had also been a pupil at West-minster School before going up to Trinity College, Cambridge, where his gifts of intelligence and personal charm won for him several prestigious positions and offered him the choice of several distinguished careers. As it happened he became a clergyman and was made Rector of Bemerton, a small parish near Salisbury. None of his poetry was published during his lifetime and he died at the age of forty. But he was to inspire many readers and writers in the years to come and it is easy to see why William Cowper found in George Herbert such a consoling companion.

Cowper's desperate plunge into poetry and religion did not, however, give him the peace and security he had hoped for. He was to be always searching, always tormented by the thought that he was eternally damned; the failed and incompetent soul he had been bullied into believing himself when at school. By the time he was thirty-two he was suffering acute anxieties about his suitability for any post offered to him and he again tried to commit suicide. But even in this the poor man lacked competence, or the necessary co-operation from fate. When he went down to the River Thames to drown himself he was rescued by a porter. When he prepared an overdose of laudanum he was saved by the arrival of his laundress. When he tried to hang himself in his bedroom he failed, three times! Perhaps fate was co-operating too much; but fortunately for a lot of people (and the hymn-books) William Cowper survived and was to live to enjoy life by the time he came to Huntingdon.

The rescue began in June 1765 when his brother John, now a Fellow at Cambridge, arranged for him to live in that nearby town on the River Ouse. At first Cowper did not like Huntingdon or its surrounding countryside. He found the fens to the north flat and boring and the local people almost as bad. In the first three months of trying to look after himself there he spent the whole of his year's allowance. Then he met the Unwin family and his life was never to be quite the same again.

Old Mr Unwin was a semi-retired clergyman and school-master with a much younger wife and two children. Although it was Unwin's son who introduced Cowper to the family it was Mrs Unwin—the Mary in Cowper's life—that the poet turned to immediately for the deep and understanding friendship he needed. In a letter to Lady Hesketh he explains his growing need of her: "I met Mrs. Unwin . . . and went home with her where we walked for nearly two hours together in the garden . . . That woman is a blessing to me and I feel every time I see her as being the better for her company."

A few months later he was to leave his own lodgings in the town and move in as a member of the Unwin family. His letters and journals show how his attitude to Huntingdon changed. " The longer I live here the better I like the place and the people who belong to it. I am now upon very good terms with no less than four families, beside two or three old scrambling fellows like myself."

The loneliness disappeared for a while, the countryside began to appeal, and the River Ouse particularly attracted him. " It is the most agreeable circumstance in this part of the world. A noble stream to bathe in, and I shall make use of it three times a week."

So much for love. Cowper suddenly makes his life sound well organized and clearly took a more positive view of the world now from the security of family life; something he had not know since his mother's death when he was only six years old.

Living in Huntingdon with the Unwin family Cowper was again able to re-examine his troubled Christian faith, and to partake again in family worship. In many ways the daily life of prayer and services at the Unwins' house can be likened to that of the Ferrar family at Little Gidding. Never a day passed without morning and evening services, and there were always Bible-readings after meals. For Cowper it was a chance to mature in tranquillity, until Mrs Unwin's husband was thrown from his horse two years later, fractured his skull and died. The accident brought back to Cowper all his previous anxieties and he worried over the prospect of having to find another home and of not seeing Mary so often.

His affection for Mrs Unwin had been no secret even though she always referred to her poet as Mr Cowper. She was also several years older than her guest so that her widowhood did not immediately present Cowper with the prospect of a closer relationship or marriage. Mr Unwin's death, in fact, was to mean the end of their life together in Huntingdon, even though the ageing clergyman had specifically expressed the wish that the young poet would stay on as a member of the family.

It took another understanding clergyman—the Reverend John Newton of Olney—to appreciate both Mrs Unwin's and William Cowper's dilemma. He invited them to stay with him in Olney as his guests and, later, as residents in his own house. The Huntingdon years were over, the Olney years were about to begin—the years during which Cowper was to write nearly one hundred hymns, including the still famous " Oh for a closer walk with God " and " God moves in a mysterious way His wonders to perform ".

Happiness, however, was a different matter and, after a few years of evangelical zeal, Cowper suffered another breakdown and a prolonged period of insanity.

Was his relationship with Mary Unwin part of the cause? He was certainly agitated and perplexed at the thought of continuing to live with Mary without asking her to marry him. But did he want marriage? As much as he loved her, as much as he wanted to share his life with her, the fear of his own weakness, instability, inadequacy, incompetence and selfishness, persuaded him that marriage was a partnership and compromise he could not meet.

Nevertheless it was still Mary on whom he relied to nurse him back to health, and it was she who saved him from self-destruction and the lunatic asylum by sitting with him day and night for several months until her own health broke.

The rest of Cowper's life is outside the area of this book and the major poems were still to be written, but the Huntingdon years made that poetry possible and it was at Huntingdon that the poet enjoyed some of the happiest days of his life. Fame, fortune and beautiful women were to come to him in middle-age, and by 1785 he was considered as the major poet of his time. But the tenderness he had known in the Unwin household between 1765 and 1767 was what he cherished most and he never forgot the woman who had made it all possible.

Mary Unwin, alas, was not able to share in his success. Her declining health led to a series of strokes in 1791 that finally left her paralysed and out of her mind.

Cowper's own tribute to her was expressed in many beautiful lines but surely none more lovely or heart-felt than

> Thy needles, once a shining store,
> For my sake restless heretofore,
> Now rust disused and shine no more,
>   My Mary.
> For though thou gladly wouldst fulfil
> The same kind office for me still,
> Thy sight now seconds not thy will,
>   My Mary.
> But well thou play'dst the housewife's part
> And all thy threads with magic art
> Have wound themselves about this heart,
>   My Mary.

Thy indistinct expressions seem
Like language uttered in a dream;
Yet me they charm, whate'er the theme,
          My Mary.
Thy silver locks once auburn bright
Are still more lovely in my sight
Than golden beams of orient light,
          My Mary.
For could I view nor them nor thee
What sight worth seeing could I see?
The sun would rise in vain for me.
          My Mary.

In 1795 Cowper had accepted a friend's invitation to move with Mrs Unwin to East Dereham in Norfolk, in the slender hope that her health would improve. Eighteen months later Mary was dead. She was buried secretly (rather like Mary Stuart), without mourners, by torchlight, in Dereham church. Cowper never mentioned her name again. Four years later he was buried by her side, his reputation as a poet virtually forgotten, remembered only for years afterwards by such understanding souls as John Clare.

And now the traffic of Huntingdon roars by. The commuters rush off to catch their morning trains and return home again in the evening, tired out and frustrated with the pressures of their world. Any Cowpers among them, I wonder?

There might be, but it's certainly a different Huntingdon to which they return to find the solace of their Mary. Oliver Cromwell, Samuel Pepys, William Cowper and Mrs Unwin are now all part of the town's history. But, again, history is not something that we can cut off and parcel into ' the Past '. We too belong to history, are part of history and continue to make history. An awareness of this continuity helps to put all things into perspective and makes life something that has no beginning and no end.

What, I wonder, will the future write about us, our towns, our battles, our poets, our love-stories and our time? The great events as we see them might only get two lines while other happenings we have ignored will take up pages.

Well, when I decided that Huntingdon would be one of my stopping-places in this journey through summer, someone said to me: " If you find anything good to say about the place I'll be surprised."

I suppose if you look at the place on any ordinary day of the week it can look ' ordinary '; but a town that has seen so much history cannot be without interest. I shall certainly remember one very sunny day (in more ways than one) when I had an unexpected lunch at The Falcon and later strolled into an Oxfam shop where I picked up two first editions of Henry Williamson, at 10p each!

*   *   *

Just outside Huntingdon town, and only a stone's throw from the railway station, is Hinchingbrooke House, one of the great historic houses in the county and more interesting than most because of its continuing history.

The house, whose beginnings can be traced back to the twelfth century, is now the Sixth Form Centre of Hinchingbrooke School and belongs to the County Council. It provides elegant assembly rooms, classrooms, private study rooms, a magnificent library and a common room for nearly two hundred students and is withstanding more pressure now than at any other period of its long life.

Through my friend Rod Stratford (one of the sixth form masters) I was able to enjoy a one-man tour of the house in the company of Liz, Sarah and Julia—three Upper Sixth girls who proved to be efficient and enthusiastic guides. They were in no doubt about what the place means to them, finishing their school life in a house that is beautiful and full of historical associations. The ornately carved doors and stairs are, after all, " different from what you'd get in an ordinary school ", said Liz, " and you do get them feeling that you're just living in a very lovely house and it's a bit like being at home." The fireplaces and decorated ceilings, the spacious windows and parklands do not, it's true, usually come with the starker, concrete schools of today. Ancient cedar trees, formal rose-gardens, secret arbours and carved stone pillars are luxuries which present-day architects have to do without. So Hinchingbrooke is different, most of the students know it's different, and I was eager to learn from them something of the rich history associated with their school.

Once upon a time—and what better way to begin a history lesson as well as a story—there was a Priory of St James, a small and poor nunnery that started its life at Eltisley soon after the Norman Conquest. In about 1200 it moved to what is now called Hinchingbrooke, where an earlier church had

already been established. Some of that early building remains
to this day and you can also see a thirteenth-century lancet
window. You can also see the stone coffins of two nuns who
were buried there at about the same time.

When the trapdoors in the floor were opened for me to see
these coffins, with their bones, I must say it was like looking
into some kind of time-machine and staring back into the past.
Did those bones really once kneel and pray here? Did that jaw-
bone and those teeth really belong to a nun 700 years ago? Liz
explained to me a theory for the larger, oval-shaped head-space
in one of the coffins. " We believe that she was perhaps the
Prioress and was buried in her coif as a sign of her superiority."

At the time of the Dissolution the revenue from surrounding
lands amounted to little more than £17 and, apart from a few
internal squabbles, life at the nunnery appears to have been a
fairly tranquil and uneventful interlude between birth and death.

It is, however, as a country house rather than a nunnery that
Hinchingbrooke has any fame, even though the shape of the
house and its materials depended very much on the remains of
that religious establishment.

Eventually, in 1538, the property passed into the ownership
of the Cromwell family, notably Richard Cromwell (alias
Williams), nephew of Thomas Cromwell. As well as the
Hinchingbrooke estate Richard also acquired the priories of
Huntingdon and St Neots, plus the abbeys of Sawtry and
Ramsey—yet another link in the intriguing story of land ownership in the fens. It is estimated that Richard Cromwell's annual
income from these properties alone was £2,500, no mean sum of
money for more than 450 years ago. It helped him to entertain
Elizabeth I on a lavish scale, even by his extravagant standards,
and the family fortune was certainly shaky after her visit.

When Henry Cromwell inherited the house he had a
gateway from Ramsey Abbey removed to Hinchingbrooke to
give the entrance to his house a little more dignity. The
gateway has two figures of ' The Green Man ' complete with
suit of leaves and a hefty club, looking fiercesomely more
pagan than Christian. It was to be Henry's honour and favour-
seeking opportunity to entertain James I and, once again, the
hospitality was generous to the point of pretentiousness.

The house stayed in the Cromwell family until 1627 and
there are several portraits of the famous member of the

family, the nephew and Lord Protector himself, warts and all.

The Hinchingbrooke estate was then sold to the Montagu family and they were responsible for a lot of rebuilding, redesigning and restoration. They were, in fact, to own the house for the next 335 years, and it is that period of its history which is particularly interesting.

Edward Montagu, son of the first Montagu owner, inherited the house in 1644. Three years later Charles I was to spend a night or two there as a prisoner of the army. These were troubled years with allegiances changing according to the dangers, but Edward proved himself to be a wise, diplomatic and astute statesman and after the restoration of the monarchy he became Earl of Sandwich, acquiring enough money to begin the major alterations to Hinchingbrooke, including the installation of five new marble fireplaces at the cost of £1,250. These are no longer there.

The Earl was also a competent sea-faring man and won distinction in his naval battles with the Dutch. Episodes of this period of his life are shown in the glass windows by William Peckitt, now to be seen in the library, windows which are, in fact, the Montagu family tree. The Star of the Garter was clearly a proud achievement and is emphasized in the windows and the portraits of the Earl.

Room after room reveals extraordinary reminders of these families' histories and in the library I was especially excited by the magnificently carved doors, the two carved wooden fireplaces, some of the original library shelves with figures from Ramsey Abbey, and the superb bow window which looks out on to the lawns and the Cedars of Lebanon.

" You see that grassy bank near that boundary wall," says one of the boys who has temporarily joined the touring party, " that's known as Pepys's Terrace because he used to walk up and down there when he came to visit the family."

Samuel Pepys was, it is true, another famous and regular visitor to Hinchingbrooke and recorded his impressions of the house in several of his diary entries. When the alterations were completed he wrote: " The house is most excellently finished and brave rooms, and good pictures, so that it do please me infinitely." It pleased him too that he had been consulted from time to time about the house.

John Montagu, the fourth Earl of Sandwich, brought his

own rich style of entertaining to Hinchingbrooke and was liberal in his hospitality. According to Charles Butler, the house " was filled with rank, beauty and talent, and everyone was at his ease ". Singers, musicians and brilliant conversationalists were all brought here to entertain, though the Earl himself " had not the least real ear for music and was equally insensible of harmony or melody ".

The fourth earl also encouraged and sponsored Captain Cook's explorations to the Pacific and Australasia, having several places named after him.

On 22 January 1830 tragedy struck the house in the form of a fire which could not be brought under control and within hours some of the finest rooms at Hinchingbrooke had been destroyed; priceless furniture and irreplaceable paintings lay scorched and beyond repair on the lawns, much of the painted glass was shattered, and sightseers walked off with what they salvaged.

But once again the house was restored and Hinchingbrooke rose again to have a distinguished life in the county. Other monarchs were to be amongst the guests, including Edward VII, and today the grounds and house retain an atmosphere that is truly compelling.

Having shown me most of the rooms, the beautiful staircase, the ornate ceilings, the original refectory and a haunted room, the girls took me on a tour of the gardens. The sun was very warm, the grass emerald, the creeper on the walls just turning crimson, the light on the old brick was warm with memories and it did not need much imagination to see Samuel Pepys walking under the shade of the cedar trees. We walked through the rose-garden, saw the Wendy House, went down towards the Nun's Bridge and back to the house for lunch. Not roast venison or boar's head, not even pheasant or jugged hare, but good old shepherd's pie and chips.

As I left Hinchingbrooke pop-music was coming loudly from the students' common room, part of the original nunnery, part of a once stately home. For some, I suppose, today's minstrels might have sounded out of place. But in another 500 years' time perhaps today's pounding rhythms will sound quaint and melancholic; after all, the lyrics are almost the same as those of 400 years ago—lost love, unrequited love, betrayed love, or simply " I love yer, baby!" They just didn't have amplified lutes or vibes in 1577.

Hinchingbrooke House became a school in 1970 but is open to the public on most summer Sundays and Bank Holiday afternoons.

*   *   *

Not far from Hinchingbrooke is the small village of Brampton, a place that has had long and involved associations with the Pepys family. For centuries they had grazed and ploughed this land on the edge of the fens, and for 250 years had served the abbey at Crowland in all its clerical and agricultural needs. They had been reeves, rent-collectors, haywards, granators, and skilled administrators, and by the fifteenth century had grown to be a family of great importance in the area. After the Dissolution of the monasteries they established manors in Cottenham, Impington, Huntingdon, Kimbolton and Brampton, experiencing mixed fortunes in both farming and marriages.

In 1601, a third son was born to the Pepys family then living at Impington and he was named John—after one of his more prosperous uncles. As he grew older the boy began to feel that the district was getting a little overcrowded with Pepyses and, even more frustrating, he could not find any interest in the family's tradition of farming. So, at the age of fourteen, he set off for London and became an apprentice tailor. When he was twenty-four, and with his own small shop, he married Margaret Kite, the sister of a Whitechapel butcher. Margaret, apparently, was a tempestuous girl who had been a wash-maid and there were quite a few domestic scenes above the tailor's shop at the end of a hard day's work. Nevertheless, she bore John Pepys eleven children, the fifth of these being Samuel, who was born on 23 February 1633. Eight days later the child was baptised in St Bride's Church and spent his early childhood growing up in Shakespeare's London full of Falstaffs, taverns, whores, squalor, riches, bear-dancing and beheadings. It was a growing city of noise, trade, travellers and excitement. Along the skyline ran the spires and bell-towers of 109 churches. Beneath the shadows of those churches was a competitive and commercial world of shopkeepers, craftsmen, masters and money-changers. The nave of St Paul's itself was used as a market for hiring servants and labourers, for borrowing and lending. Coaches and horses clattered through the narrow streets, and the Thames stank with the city's filth.

Far beyond London lay the green countryside of Cambridgeshire and Huntingdonshire, the countryside that Samuel's
father had left at the age of fourteen. There were still relatives
living in the area, including an uncle at Huntingdon and an uncle
at Brampton. At the age of ten Samuel was sent to stay with his
relations in Huntingdon and attended the local grammar school,
the school where Oliver Cromwell had also been a pupil.

Pepys enjoyed the rural life and took a particular liking to
his Uncle Robert at Brampton, helping him with his accounts
and correspondence. Robert Pepys also took to his youngest
nephew and was, eventually, to bequeath his estate to him
rather than to his nearer relatives. It was a bequest that was to
lead Samuel into several long and bitter legal battles with
other members of the family, incurring for a time costs that
were greater than the value of the inheritance which, he
discovered, carried quite a few debts as well.

By the middle of 1663, however, the wrangles of two years
came to an end, settlements were agreed upon, and the
Brampton estate passed to Samuel's father John until his
death, and thereafter to Samuel himself. John Pepys took up
residence later that year and Samuel (with his wife Elizabeth)
were to visit the manor on several occasions.

Brampton became a retreat from the political rows and noise
of London, a refuge from the enemies in the Admiralty and the
gossip, of Fleet Street. By 1667 it also became a welcome
sanctuary from the conspiracies in the city and the national bank-
ruptcy that preceded the Dutch invasion. Having survived
plague and fire, Pepys did not relish surviving revolution or being
taken prisoner. On 13 June he sent his wife and father (who'd
been visiting him) back to Brampton with more than £1,300 in
gold, followed by a clerk with a further £1,000. For safety the
money was buried in the garden during morning service on the
following Sunday—a security measure that worried Pepys not
a little when he heard of it from his clerk. It worried him even
more when, on arrival at Brampton in October, his wife said
she could not remember exactly in which part of the garden she
had buried their fortune. By the light of a lantern her husband
began digging feverishly until he found the damp bags and all
the contents. Once more he was saved, and Brampton breathed
again.

But I wonder, did he find it all?

5

"No Country for Old Men . . ."

A July Saturday and the world is going on holiday—or so it appears. The streets are solid with people in vulgar vests and provocative dresses. The roads are so congested with cars and caravans that the traffic-jams to the west country make the headlines in the television news, as they do each year when the British public decides that it's got to be summer. The railway stations are almost as bad and look worse because there always seems to be far more luggage than people.

I'm only going to Cambridge—thirty-five miles away—but I've decided to go by rail rather than get caught in traffic-jams and then have nightmares trying to find a convenient car-park for a fortnight. With all its drawbacks on a hot day like this I still enjoy a train journey. I can't agree with John Ruskin who said: " Going by railroad I do not consider as travelling at all; it is merely being ' sent ' to a place and is very little different from becoming a parcel."

But surely you make of a journey what you want to make of it. I suppose you could make a voyage round the world boring, if you wanted to. Train journeys are far from boring, especially if you're curious about your fellow travellers. Even if you're not you can still sit back and read a book, or lean forward and write a letter, or even a novel if the journey takes that long or your train is delayed—it has been done, though I admit it took more than one journey. If none of these pastimes appeal you can just relax, look out of the window and let someone else worry about the driving.

I'm a compulsive looker-out-of-windows traveller and, however familiar the journey, I still can't resist staring out of this world-on-wheels, hoping for something different.

I was surprised to find out recently how many children had never been on a train. In one school I visited only one girl in a class of twenty-eight had actually been on a train journey. Some had not even been to a station. They had been on jumbo jets, and 707s, expensive liners, camels, elephants, and rickshaws. But not trains. And why? Because they had all grown up, of course, in an age where the family car was a natural part of life, like the television, the telephone, the freezer. What a pity they won't know the excitement of waiting at their local stations for the train to arrive that will speed them off to a marvellous holiday in Hunstanton or Cromer!

My train pulls in—on time—and I find a seat on the side of the compartment where I think I'll get the best view, and I always feel I've made the wrong choice.

Today I am going to Cambridge, not on holiday, but to take part in the annual W.E.A. Summer School to be held at St John's College. I ought to be reading the unread books, preparing myself mentally for a fortnight's word-bashing, but the landscape really does look good today. It's too seductive to spend all the time looking at books. The fields drowse under the heat's haze, as contented as someone who has fed or loved well. Satisfied, sleepy, and inexpressibly happy. Fields can look happy, I'm sure of it—though I'm always being told that fields can't express anything because they have no consciousness. Do you always have to be conscious to express something? I wonder.

I watch the fields and enjoy again their *feeling* of joy and fulfilment as they close their eyes and half-doze in the afternoon heat. Acres of cereals, potatoes, sugar-beet, carrots; and then, a sudden moment of life as the water-sprayers spin slowly round over a field of celery, each spray creating its own rainbow—twenty rainbows in all.

The train passes Welney and there is a mysterious quality about the marshes, deeper than sleep, older than the crops. A month ago they were still under water following a very wet spring. Now the grass and wild flowers have returned and the cattle graze on the thick grass. One heron is being pursued, or attacked, by another—two old-fashioned bi-planes engaged in a dog-fight, or bird-fight!

As the train approaches Ely the cathedral slowly appears out of the haze like a brass-rubbing taking shape. In the hidden river the bright sails of sailing-boats cut like shark's fins through the watery landscape. One sail is bigger than the

Holywell, near St Ives

Cowper House, Huntingdon, where the poet William Cowper lived

Cromwell Museum, Huntingdon, once the grammar school where
Oliver Cromwell and Samuel Pepys were pupils

The courtyard of the George Hotel, Huntingdon

The Bridge of Sighs, St John's College, Cambridge

By the River Cam, Cambridge

King's College Chapel, Cambridge

The American War Cemetery, Madingley, near Cambridge

Harvesting on land once owned by George Borrow

Gathering celery in the fens

Downham Market clock-tower

Swaffham Market Place and Buttercross

Swaffham churchyard

rest—a *Moby Dick* white sail that suddenly disappears behind a clump of willow trees. Water-lilies break up the reflections in a tributary and the surface looks like a big jigsaw-puzzle with pieces missing. And then the river comes into view. The train pulls into the station, exchanges one lot of luggage for another and sets off on the last few miles to Cambridge.

If it had not been for the familiar buildings I would have wondered if I'd arrived at the right place. Cambridge more and more seems to be taken over by the tourists in summer. French, German, Italian, American, Norwegian, Greek and Japanese, a colossal aviary of tongues, all twittering away over street-maps, guide-books and itineraries, a summer Babel of sightseers, a Gargantuan mixed salad of accents and costumes, rucksacks and transistors, cultures and expectations, questions and cameras. A million feet wearing away the pavements by inches, as many shoulders inflicting a million bruises as the crowds try to separate themselves into those coming and those going, and the camera-shutters clicking so furiously you'd think the world had been taken over by amplified grass-hoppers. Day after day the crowds descend, all here to see a place made famous by the famous—and, oh, how those famous would hate it, not least William Wordsworth, who was once a student at St John's—

> The world is too much with us; late and soon,
> Getting and spending, we lay waste our powers:
> Little we see in Nature that is ours;
> We have given our hearts away, a sordid boon!

*   *   *

A Summer School at least gets you *inside* the colleges and away from the sordid boon. It gives you the nights in Cambridge too, as well as the days; and the nights can be pure magic.

Everyone has arrived now; we have received our orders, have been directed to our rooms and, in the morning, the School will begin in earnest. The subject is *Language and the Creative Imagination*: if it doesn't work here it never will.

From my fourth-floor window in New Court—which is, incidentally, already nearly 150 years old—I look out over the cloisters, the almost sacred lawns, and the ridges of trees that stretch away into the distance. The River Cam flows quietly away beneath the willows and beeches, carrying its slender punts like driftwood into the shadows of a bridge. The skyline is dominated by the roof and crenellations of King's College Chapel and the Wren Library. The martins weave their own intricate pattern in the humid air. They are like unwanted snowflakes with black wings, afraid to settle in case they melt.

It grows darker. The trees disappear. The college clocks chime out their quarter-hours—a healing sound to tired ears—and then the floodlights come on to continue the beauty of stone. Down below, the arches of the cloisters are transformed into stained-glass windows by the floodlights shining through the foliage and flowers of that always beautiful border-garden.

Then, from the river, comes the sound of madrigals and the night is suddenly made into a world for lovers. You won't believe it, but the moon is shining and owls are calling from the hidden trees. I feel I ought to be reading aloud in my empty room W. B. Yeats's poem.

> That is no country for old men. The young
> In one another's arms . . .

for there is something of Byzantium about this night, an artistic perfection where the ideal is achieved and nothing decays; where youth and love exist, never to die.

But I console myself with the fact that I have seen quite a few old men tottering back to their rooms after dinner and port, so I will stay here and envy the young who know how to make the night theirs. Who knows; by the end of the fortnight I may have rediscovered the secret.

One day, two days, and the first week is already ticking by, intense with lectures, discussions, seminars, tutorials, illustrated talks, arguments, reading and writing, all kinds of skills demonstrated in stories and poems about Welsh miners, eccentric doctors, East Anglian farm-workers, the Potteries, village funerals, a special encounter in Delhi, and a score of other subjects competing so much with the attractions of this city that there has not been much chance to venture out into the town to look at the rest of Cambridge, yet. It is also festival time and occasionally you get snatches of the fun being had outside. I hear the distant sound of carnival parades, the persistent drum-beats and the liberated laughter, all emphasizing the riches of summer. Morris-dancers and pipers meet on the grass, the rhythmic jingle of their music older than stone.

Today ends with a fierce, low light gilding the tops of trees and the ornate stone of Kings. Green and white tinged with gold. The grass is momentarily drowned under pools of light which soak dramatically into the ground as a cloud covers the sun, leaving the lawns darker than before. Each time I look up from my desk there is a different pattern in the sky. And always the martins, the St John's martins, in their rapid bat-like flitting through the air, tumbling like punctuation marks—commas in flight, looking for phrases on which to settle.

And always, not very far away, the secret laughter of the young and the persuasive talk of those who, for a while, live in a fantasy world that they will always think of as reality. Perhaps it is. Why not be romantic once in a while and believe it all to be true. The fantasy may well be the dull reality to which many of these students will return, not a dream but a nightmare.

* * *

However crowded, noisy, congested and uncomfortable Cambridge can be in summer it is still a city you cannot ignore. With all the changes that have gone on over the years there can be few cities in Europe that can offer more to the romantic—or, for that matter, to the realist. Art galleries, museums, bookshops, churches, colleges, immortalized walks and buildings, the Backs and the river. It's a beautiful city, preserving the old, creating the new, respecting most of its past, making way for the future. It is many things to many people. It is a city that draws people from all over the world. Millions of words have been written about it—as the local bookshops will testify with their bewildering stacks of glossy books, local guides, histories, memoirs, lavishly illustrated volumes for coffee tables, pamphlets and sundry publications.

You may say, then why add more? And quite honestly I don't think I should, but how can you ignore Cambridge when there is so much to offer?

I think that one needs to be reminded too that there was life in Cambridge long before the university arrived in the thirteenth century. A Roman settlement existed here for many years on Castle Hill and the Danes wintered here in 875. The town was burnt down in 1010 but was rebuilt and became well known for its market before the Norman Conquest. The river was busy with barges plying their trade from the Continent to the Midlands, and several religious communities were established during the eleventh and twelfth centuries.

A tour of Cambridge churches will tell you much of this early history. St Bene't's has a tower dating from 1050; St Botolph's, St Mary's and the Round Church are all of great interest.

The first mayor of the city was elected in 1231 and the existence of a number of guilds and societies emphasize the town's importance, an importance not overlooked by the rebellious students of Oxford in 1209, who left that city to find new places of learning at Cambridge and Reading.

The early years of town and gown coming together were by no means easy or harmonious. The scholars then had to find their own lodgings in private houses and there were frequent complaints of over-charging until hostels, controlled by a master, were established. Even so, the students continued to be high-spirited and rowdy, much to the annoyance of the local tradespeople. When Henry III invited students from the Continent to join the English universities, prices and rents were raised to exploit the situation, and, once again, the local scholars took their argument beyond the debating chamber. It's reassuring in a way to know that we're not the only generation guilty of exploitation. Whatever evils, corruptions, disturbances, uproars and outcries we may think are the scourges of our times today, it looks as if similar events and actions have all been gone through before, for as long as the history books can recall.

By 1279 there were still no colleges as we know them today. Learning and 'living-in' was not possible until there were buildings to accommodate such scholastic communities, or 'colleges'. Such foundations needed money and, as usual, money was not always easy to come by. There were, however, seventeen churches in the town, as well as several religious houses, and these continued to have considerable influence on the growth of Cambridge.

The history of Cambridge and the University is, of course, too long and complex to summarize in this chapter of impressions, but to know something of that history is to enhance your appreciation of the place today. It was certainly not all glamour, and the hard, spartan life lived behind those pleasant courts and cloisters was not much to envy.

I'm going to concentrate on St John's College which is, after all, my 'home' for two weeks, and where I feel much of Cambridge's past is to be realized. The old and the new certainly come together here in the most dramatic way with the very modern construction of the new Cripps building neighbouring the very old stone School of Pythagoras, the remains of a twelfth-century manor house (the origins of its name unknown).

St John's College, by no means the oldest college in Cambrige, was founded in 1511 by the mother of Henry VII, the Lady Margaret Beaufort, who died before any progress had been made on the new building.

The moment you enter the first court from the noisy street you are aware of an immediate stepping-back into a history of learning and tradition. In those early years of the College students would come up, at the remarkably young age of thirteen, to study theology, philosophy, logic, mathematics, Greek and, in some cases, medicine. Accommodation was far from lavish, the young students sharing not only rooms but also beds. (Despite all the rumours that go around, this is not a common practice on Summer Schools.) For those earlier students the day began at 4 a.m. Private prayers and Mass were said before 6 a.m. and the junior members then had two hours of lectures before a break for food. There was a period of leisure after lunch, but lectures resumed at 3 p.m. until supper. Discipline was, by today's standards, severe! You could, for instance, find yourself on a bread-and-water diet for speaking English instead of Latin, or you could expect a whipping for disobeying an order, or get expelled for theft, treason or adultery—an unlikely crime, surely, for such young students!

St John's Chapel, built in 1866–9, breaks your imaginative link with the sixteenth century and is an addition to the College that has received its fair share of criticism over the years. But if you forget the over-imposing tower and think more of the beautiful sound created inside by the excellent chapel choir, all can be forgiven. St John's has a long tradition of music, matching its friendly rivals down the road. It has had a choir since 1670 and is famous today throughout the world for its superb recordings, recitals and broadcasts. I shall always associate it with a memorable performance of Faure's *Requiem*, that lovely ' water-colour ' of requiems, a work which, strangely enough, was to feature again this year in my memories of Cambridge.

Before leaving the first court, stop for a moment at staircase F, and remember that it was here that the young William Wordsworth lived from 1789 to 1791 when he was a student. Another scholar who became famous was William Wilberforce.

Towards the end of the sixteenth century the second court was added and a feature of this is the Fellows' Combination Room, with its beautiful plaster ceiling and wood panelling. It is a room that speaks of elegance and profound conversation. In contrast to *its* splendour there is the story of the young James Wood, a poor student and son of a Lancashire weaver, who lived in a garret at the top of one of the Shrewsbury towers, where he was seen, on many occasions, sitting on the stairs with his feet wrapped in straw to keep warm, studying by a frail rushlight until late at night. Candles and fires were more than he could afford but he persevered and went on to enjoy a distinguished academic career, becoming Master and Vice-Chancellor. Which just proves what can be achieved without State grants.

Beyond the second court is the third court with its library, and beyond that the famous Bridge of Sighs which crosses the River Cam into New Court, the court where I am lucky enough to be sitting now writing this chapter.

The Bridge of Sighs was built in 1831 and, although it bears little resemblance to the more famous Venetian one, it is undoubtedly one of the main attractions of Cambridge, much photographed, much sighed over, undeniably attractive and romantic—especially at night.

From New Court you get an unparalleled view of the Backs with the lawns, gardens, river and trees. In spring the crocuses, daffodils and chestnut trees make this a memorable walk, though I think I would settle for a late evening stroll in summer when the mist is rising over the low ground and the beds of nicotiana fill the air with their exotic scent.

The stone eagle over the central archway is a regular target for pranksters and for a couple of days during our stay the proud wings have carried a bright orange plastic chair. The proud bird did not, I feel, enjoy the joke and looked rather indignant until four workmen arrived with their ladders to remove the shining saddle. One workman patted the bird on the back with familiar affection and said something like " I'm sorry old girl . . . or boy."

St John's also has the oldest rowing society on the river and its Lady Margaret Boat Club was founded in 1825. Its members wore scarlet jackets which were soon to give a new word to the English language—*blazers.*

Beyond New Court is something much newer and more startling—the latest addition to St John's College, built between 1964 and 1967, through the generosity of the Cripps Foundation, at a cost of £1½ million. It is a building that bravely moves into the twentieth century when surrounded by so much that is old. Its rooms are comfortable and its students must be grateful that they do not have to walk half a mile for a shower or a lavatory. The Cripps building at last breaks with the monastic influence of the earlier buildings and provides amenities that would have caused the eyebrows of one Fellow to rise even higher than they did in 1921 when he asked why he should support plans for a bath-house. " What do they want baths for, they're only here for eight weeks at a time?"

My own favourite spot by the river is near the steps of the Cripps building where the water is shaded by lovely trees and the new and the old are married in perfect harmony. To the right is the Bridge of Sighs, to the left is Magdalene Bridge, opposite is the Master's Lodge, behind me is the new white extension. Dates are not separated but joined by their reflection in something older than either. 1624 and 1964 themselves bridge such a short span of this city's history. In another hundred years, what? More to see? More to photograph? More and more visitors? No doubt. But those far-ahead days do not concern us this week or next.

Our first week is now more concerned about its last, rapidly melting-away hours. We have parties—official and unofficial— and try to give those hours a permanence so that they will stay in our minds longer perhaps than some of our words on the page.

The bells have whispered their midnight chimes through the night's keyhole but we do not hear. From one of the student's rooms on the top floor we look out over a world that has been transformed into a silent fantasy. The full moon opens in the middle of pale clouds like an exotic flower in a dark lake. The floodlit buildings do, I admit, look very beautiful tonight and their reflections in the river leave you with a barren vocabulary. And it's not just the workings of the wine! Others feel it too who have only been on orange joice. Down below the Bridge of Sighs is now deserted. Beneath its arch is the perfect reflection of the red walls and chimneys beyond, and the trees open like wings in the olive-green water. It is quiet, still, peaceful, unreal and, thankfully, outside the limitation of Time or language. The date on the wall facing us says 1624—and it is! Tomorrow there will be courtesans and sweet music, leisure and learning, love and a different summer. If the night is real, then surely tomorrow cannot belong to the twentieth century and sad departings. The buildings, the bridges, the water and the reflections are all far too romantic to be English—and yet they are! You could be forgiven though for thinking of Venice, Bruges or Amsterdam. Several of us feel that way about it, depending on our place of special memory. One of my students, Shirley Bridger, expressed her feelings about the scene in these lines

> Was that reality—
> Bruges in an English night?
> Or was it just a metaphor
> Fashioned in water?
> For when I try to grasp it
> It shivers a moment,
> Breaks up, and then is gone.

Perhaps we need such metaphors, and it is necessary for us to see the reflections broken if we are to hold them in memory. The momentary shiver enters into our being. But the night is never lost.

The owls, which have been a feature of our nights in Cambridge, flute again through the moonlit trees and the mist rises from the lawns, as if it, too, wishes to seal in for ever the footprints of all who have walked here, preserving in vapour and shadow the people who have shared joy, love, and the secrets of strangers—" the young in one another's arms ".

But reality has a different meaning in the morning and we

know that we cannot hold on to such moonlit hours for ever; only in the words and memories that we have tried to perfect, and the imaginations we have tried to improve, can we keep such moments alive!

The first week ends and a new group of students arrive; the lectures and work all have to be gone through again, but with different personalities, different problems, different relationships. The festival ends. The floodlights are switched off. The melodies of Don McLean, sung for us very beautifully by Paul Burgon, haunt the mind. The second week is over too, and the partings and promises are gone through again, the taxis ordered for the start of the journeys back—to where, or what, or whom?

It's still surprising how sad one can be at saying goodbye to people you've only known for a week—not only people, but a place. C. Day Lewis expressed it well when he wrote

> Nothing so sharply reminds a man he is mortal
> As leaving a place . . .

We all become mortals again as we set off in different directions and the different landscapes absorb us once more into the easy ordinariness of the rest of the year. We are alone again with the familiar. 1624, 1977 . . . does it matter?

*   *   *

The train takes me back again over the fens. I sit back and sigh with relief. Ah, those fields! That light! What a respite! What a cure for the eyes after the crowds, the millions of faces, the streets, the stones, the millions of words, the concentration, listening and staring! What an escape from history, tradition, dates, rules, studying, discipline and talking. Now there is nothing that needs analysing, criticizing, marking or praising. The fields can be enjoyed for themselves alone. I chant a new psalm to myself: Look at that wheat, that celery, those beans. Look at the river, the grass and the shining greens. Look at that space, the telegraph poles, the dykes and the cows. Look at the farms, the familiar landmarks, a favourite house. And of course home has something to do with the relief and the ecstasy of the return journey. The rhythm of the wheels and the native horizon quickens the pulse. Not long now and it will all be over, and I can rest at last; throw down the brief-cases and watch telly all day.

Don't get me wrong. I did enjoy myself in that other world, truly! I might even do it again—one day.

POSTSCRIPT

For the thousands who cannot enjoy a fortnight ' living-in ', or who want to see more than one college, Cambridge does, of course, offer many other treasures. The Fitzwilliam Museum, for instance, has a marvellous collection of paintings, drawings, prints, illuminated manuscripts, coins, pottery, porcelain and jade. There is also the Folk Museum with its fascinating collection of items from East Anglia's past, and Kettles Yard Art Gallery.

Beyond Cambridge, but very much associated with it, is Grantchester, which may not have been so sought after had Rupert Brooke not written a poem about it. The poem itself isn't at all flattering about most of the surrounding villages and Grantchester's popularity rests solely on two tongue-in-cheek lines that ask

> . . . yet
> stands the church clock at ten to three?
> And is there honey still for tea?

The answer to the first part of the question is " No ", and to the second, " Yes "—well, sort of . . . and Brooke might well raise a quizzical, or cynical, eye at that.

To walk to Grantchester over the meadows is the traditional way and, if you get there in time for lunch you can get good bar snacks at one of the locals, or, if you arrive in time for tea then you can have your cream and honey under the apple trees of the Orchard Garden; wasps and all if it's fairly late in the season. The secret is not to annoy these pests by trying to swat them but to invite them to have tea with you by liberally spreading one of your slices of bread and butter with jam, or honey, and then placing it on a spare chair. The wasps soon get the message and leave you and your table alone.

Another place of interest on the outskirts of Cambridge is the American Military Cemetery at Madingley. A silent, shattering experience of the cost of war. The crescent rows of white crosses mark the graves of 3,811 military dead, and the roll-call on The Wall of the Missing records the names of 5,125 servicemen whose graves are unknown—a pitiful reminder of what our peace, our privileges and our present existence have cost. It is a scene that can, sadly, be multiplied many times throughout Europe. The reminder here is made with dignity and respect on a beautiful slope of English soil. If these things are enough to show regret and to express gratitude, then Madingley surely succeeds. It is a moving experience to stand on the steps of the Memorial Chapel or at the foot of the 72-foot flagpole from where you can see Ely Cathedral sixteen miles away. But, however tastefully prepared, a war cemetery is also " no country for old men " and the thousands of dates on the thousands of crosses have an angry silence about them. Wilfred Owen spoke for the victims of all wars and for all generations when he wrote

> Was it for this the clay grew tall?
> O what made fatuous sunbeams toil
> To break earth's sleep at all?

6

Mainly Horses and Other Fine Folk

Sometimes, once in a while, there are days which arrive on the morning doorstep—before the milkman or the post—days of such promise and unpredictability that you know there is nothing you can do but surrender to them. Often they are days of deliverance; deliverance from anxieties, stalemate, aches, pains and hindrances that would make staying indoors unbearable.

The sun of course makes a difference and when I awoke this morning it was already striding as loud and shining as a brass band across my room. It was saying " Get up, rouse yourself, get in step . . . we're going out and today things are going to happen!"

So what could I do but respond with the same degree of energy and positive enthusiasm. One look at the sky and I knew it was a day to leap into, as you might leap into a pool of blue water; a day to lock the doors on a house and enjoy again the freedom of instincts.

*   *   *

I leave the city, cross the Nene as usual, and follow my nose into the fens through Farcet and Yaxley. I get the feeling it's a day for calling on friends, people I've not met all that often but who are so warm and generous that they qualify for friendship after just a few meetings.

I'm thinking now of several good people I know who are the salt of the earth; sincere, honest, homely folk who have lived in the same villages all their lives, who have worked on the same farms for years and whose knowledge of the land is encyclopaedic. They are to be found in almost any fen village and I have been privileged to be taken into their homes and to share the memories of their lives with them.

I pull in for a moment at the edge of a field where the wheat harvest is still being gathered in and feel a strong sense of continuity emanating from the earth. These fields have, I know, been worked for generations by the same families working for the same farming families—men, women, children, master and servant.

I think particularly of people like Mrs Ivy Dow and her husband, or Mr Sam Briggs, or Gordon Mason; people who have carried on from their fathers, who have cared for the land, who have worked it, protected it, seen it change and still love it. It isn't a rural sentimentality because these people have known too well all the hardships of a life on the land; but it is a genuine feeling of respect and involvement, of experience and love, that they express.

Thinking about these men and women I feel that my instinct has brought me into the fens today because I want to be with them, to know again that enrichment. I decide to call on Mrs Dow. She isn't expecting me. It might not be a convenient time. But we'll see.

I make my way through the back garden gate, tap on the open door and call good morning.

"Good Lord, look who's here! Come on in."

Immediately all the jobs are put aside and I am invited into her small sitting-room.

"Sit down . . . it's a long time since we saw you."

I'm glad to be back. The black-lead grate is nursing a sleeping fire. The walls are shining with the many gleaming horse-brasses. There are pictures of horses, memories of horses, photograph albums full of horses. In fact Mrs Dow loves horses, talks horses, *lives* horses. She has worked with horses all her life, from the day she left school at thirteen. By the time she was fourteen she had her own team and was doing a man's work for one-and-sixpence a day.

The horses' names come back to her as clearly as if she'd just fed them—Brownie, Bonnie, Flower, Short, Prince, Daisy, Major and Smart, and the family pony Bob.

The clock ticks on the mantelpiece. The budgie heckles from his cage. The dog, Tammy, demands attention. The sun flows through the kitchen window and door. I relax in the fireside chair and the talk begins to gather pace.

Photographs from the 1920s and '30s are brought out and I

hear again of the fascinating life these people have lived on the
land, always in the same fens, always making the most of what
life had to offer. Sometimes it wasn't very much, at least not
financially, and there was often a struggle to make ends
meet.

" But we've never owed anybody a penny all our married
lives, have we?" says Mrs Dow to her husband. " We've known
hard times and good times but we've always lived within our
means, and I think we've been as happy and as contented as
anyone."

Looking through the photograph albums again I remember
the first time I met Mrs Dow. It was at the local Women's
Institute—that splendid organization that does so much to
preserve the customs, characters and histories of the country.
Two days later I was sitting in this room recording part of a
programme for the B.B.C. It was an interview which suddenly
produced an old ploughing song which Mrs Dow used to sing
to her horses when she wanted a good day's work out of them.

> *Down in the field where the buttercups grow*
> *I loved Mary Green and she loved me so,*
> *She thought I was slow till I let myself go,*
> *Down in the fields where the buttercups grow.*
>
> *Down in the field where the buttercups grow,*
> *As I made love to Mary beside a haystack*
> *A bumble bee flew down the small of her back,*
> *Down in the field where the buttercups grow.*
>
> *Down in the field where the buttercups grow*
> *I tried to help Mary as I saw her distress,*
> *So I plunged my hand down the front of her dress,*
> *Down in the field where the buttercups grow.*
>
> *Down in the field where the buttercups grow*
> *I walked with my Mary all through the long grass,*
> *And the nettles grew sideways to let us go past,*
> *Down in the field where the buttercups grow.*
>
> *Down in the field where the buttercups grow*
> *A cow licking Mary's face tickled her so,*
> *She thought it was me and said "don't slobber, Joe!"*
> *Down in the field where the buttercups grow.*

Well after that, and her very successful contribution to my
radio programme, I knew that I should not lose touch with Mrs

Dow and, over a relatively short period of time, we have, I think, got to know each other fairly well.

Sitting here in her house again I feel I have known her and her husband for a long time. The talk flows easily. The memories come hurrying back.

We return to the photographs of the horses.

" That's Bob. He were a lovely pony. My father bought him at Peterborough Horse Fair for £8 before the First World War. Lovely animal he was. Intelligent, and a mind of his own. Mind you, mother wasn't too pleased when father brought him home, not with thirteen of us children to feed. 'What d'you want to spend your hard-earned savings on a pony for when we can do with the money in the house?' But old Bob more than repaid that £8. Worked like a farm-horse he did all the week, and took the family out in the trap at the weekends. During the First World War my sister used to meet the local boys home on leave and bring them from Peterborough station to Yaxley, and take them back again when their time was up—as it often was for them in more ways than one, poor things . . . I've done every kind of land work you can think of, everything— ploughing, drilling, rolling, harrowing, harvest, threshing, stacking, potatoes, celery, carrots—you name it, I've done it. And I've worked with some marvellous people too. Jack was a fine horse-keeper I knew, ever so gentle, a lovely man with horses . . . Mind you, not all horses are easy to handle and some could be right devils. We had one mare called Smart and she could be as temperamental as any human. I used to hate getting her in my team."

Half an hour quickly becomes an hour. One hour becomes two. I have a lesson on how to squeeze warble-flies out of bullocks (which puts me off beef for a while) and then hear of diseases and remedies I never knew existed.

From the harsher experiences of farm-work we talk about cottage life and how people provided for themselves, both in food and entertainment. We discuss the merits of making jam from rhubarb, marrow, peaches, rose-petals and elderflower. We talk about puddings (and fen-men love a good pudding) and then about chutney and pickles. There's nothing, it seems, that you cannot use for making something and put into a jar for another day.

When a few jars are produced from a dark cupboard

memories are awakened of my own grandmother's pantry smelling of jars filled with secrets and labelled with gummed paper that carried names as exotic as anything from the Garden of Sheba or the Orient.

From another cupboard Mrs Dow now produces three or four leather-bound volumes of the parish magazine from 1891 and we laugh over some of the news items of eighty years ago—choir outings to Great Yarmouth, village concerts, harvest festivals, and one paragraph where the vicar explains that the grapes could not be given as usual to the poor that year as they (the grapes) had been stolen from the pulpit during the service on Sunday.

Eventually we move out into the garden which appears to have everything they will need to see them through the winter—potatoes, cabbage, carrots, beans and onions; tomatoes and cucumbers in the greenhouse; dahlias, sweet-peas, apples, blackberries, honeysuckle and fuchsias; seeds ripening ready for next year; hens laying eggs for them; and a barn that is well stocked with logs that Mr Dow has sawn from bog-oaks that have come from out of the fen. There's not a weed to be seen where it should not be and every inch of the garden is put to use.

I express my admiration and ask Mr Dow how he still manages to work such a big piece of land.

" Oh, this is nothing. I could do with more really, to keep me busy."

These are people who have learnt the meaning of self-sufficiency and survival; a people who have learnt to live with all the seasons and make the best of their earth. There is a quality about their lives that many would envy.

When I leave, my arms are loaded with runner-beans, onions, strawberry and peach jam, a couple of country books and recipes, and many more fresh memories from life of sixty years ago.

" Call again, any time you like," they say to me at the gate. " And mind how you go."

*   *   *

I go to the other end of the village to see Mr Sam Briggs who is ninety-two, a man who can talk about horses even longer than Mrs Dow.

" I've worked with horses all my life, and my father before me, and my grandfather. I was only seven when I went out foaling with my father. He didn't want me to go but he could see I had it in me, so he made me sit on the straw and be quiet. I saw a good many foals born during the next sixty years or so. I've helped many a mare to foal, and a hard time some of 'em had too. I've had to deliver dead foals as well. Had my arm in up to my shoulder to turn the foal over and get its legs in the right position. When the mares were having a bad birth I'd sing to them . . . I was always singing . . ."

" Mrs Dow was telling me that she used to sing to her horses when she wanted them to work well. Did you sing to your horses?"

" A lot of the time, whether they were foaling or ploughing."

" What did you sing when you were in the fields?"

> *"My name is Jim the Carter*
> *A jolly boy am I,*
> *I always am contented*
> *Be the weather wet or dry . . ."*

He sings several verses, and a few other songs as well, including " Come follow the plough, boys ". When he looks up there is a faraway look in his eyes as he remembers his days as a young man.

" I had a good voice then," he says. " I was well known around here; used to sing in the church choir—went all over the fens, singing in churches and chapels, even at dinners and various meetings."

" And what did you sing then, in the churches, for instance?"

" All the old 'uns. One of my favourites was ' How Lovely Are Thy Dwellings '—do you know it?"

And suddenly, at the age of ninety-two, and still recovering from an illness, he begins, in what was clearly a once very lovely tenor voice to sing

> *"How lovely are Thy dwellings fair*
> *O Lord of Hosts . . ."*

His frail arm rises with the high notes, the arm that brought foals out of the dark into the lamplit stable. And then he stops . . .

" But I was going to tell you about the ploughing. When I had a good team I never used a rein. Did it all by word of

mouth—*Whoa!* and *Hoick!* And they all knew! There was
Diamond, Beauty and Bounce. Lovely animals they were. I
broke 'em in, trained 'em and worked with them for years. We
understood each other and they knew what I wanted. They
used to come to the gate to meet me in the mornings."

" How many horses were you responsible for at any one
time?"

" As many as twenty-two before the war. But then the war
came and they took some of my boys off to the trenches and
they never came back. They took some of the horses too, but
they paid for them. About £80–£100 each."

He becomes silent again for a few moments as his eyes search
far back to 1914–18 and then says " A terrible waste, boys and
horses, the best in the land. The world's never been quite the
same since."

We talk about the conditions on the land in those early days
at the turn of the century, about the good masters and the bad
masters.

" Most of them were all right, but you could never be sure
. . . they always won in the end. I was lucky to work for men who
trusted me. I only once had a row with a master and so I said to
him ' It strikes me I've worked for you too long.' So I left."

We talk about wages and the prices that some of the crops
fetched.

" I've taken cart-loads of carrots to the station that were only
fetching seven-and-sixpence a ton, and that's no fairy-tale.
What I'm telling you is the truth. I've sold twelve heads of
celery tied with willow for as little as three-ha'pence."

" What about tractors? How did you get on with them when
they came on the farms?"

He laughs quietly to himself at the thought. " The first and
only time I went on a tractor I put the blessed thing in the
dyke. The master says to me, ' Sam, you'd better stick with the
horses,' so I did. But by then my time was nearly up so it didn't
matter. I had a bad heart-attack in my early sixties and two
doctors gave me a week to live . . . It's been the longest week
I've ever known . . . No, we weren't afraid of hard work in them
days. I could drill ten acre in a morning when I was young and
still be the first back at the yard for my lunch."

Well, I certainly shan't be the first back for any kind of meal
this morning. It's already early afternoon and I make an effort

to move. But it isn't easy when you're with good country folk and there are still many more experiences to hear and more photographs to see.

When I do say goodbye I can see there are many untold stories opening like flowers in his mind, stories that may not be remembered when I see him again.

I go out on to the edge of those fields which these good people have worked. Today's crops are the offspring of their lifetime of care. The land is clean, healthy and fertile. New seeds are sown, new harvests are reaped, new generations follow the old, but you cannot forget that race of people who knew nothing else but the demands of each season, the demands of a master, and still had time for their singing.

*   *   *

It's a pull to tear myself away from this particular corner of the country today, but I drive on because there are other people I want to see.

A man with a scythe is cutting the long grass on a dykeside and suddenly a company of scarlet poppies fall, mown down; a symbolic action; the stable-lads who will not come back. The rhythm of the man's arms swing backwards and forwards like a slow pendulum counting not minutes but years.

The opposite side of the road is still bright with wild flowers. Distant houses shine as if they've just been newly white-washed. Between the rows of carrots the black soil looks as soft as baking powder. It reminds me of a letter I had a couple of years ago from a Mr Wilfred Leonard of Dersingham, a man who was born in 1892, who has a great love of the fens and some interesting stories to tell about this soft peat soil—and horses!

One day his elder brother was sent to roll a field with a team consisting of a shaft-horse and two in traces, " the middle one being a youngster in training and rather apt to be skittish at times. To ease things my brother took me with him to lead the fore-horse. All went well until I grew weary and the horse grew quiet. So my brother told me I could ride on the roller while he got on with the job, which he did ". But all of a sudden there was a cry for help and, looking round, Mr Leonard's brother saw the young boy halfway under the roller. Quick as lightning he said, "I've no belly-band! Can't back! I'll have to go on ahead and be damned!" When he stopped the team his young brother scrambled to his feet seemingly unhurt by the heavy, flat roller. His brother's comments were, apparently, typical of him. "You've got a mucky face! It's a pity we haven't got any lead so we could get a statue made of you from that hole!"

There can be few people more grateful for the soft fenland soil—which was, so I'm told, much softer and deeper sixty years ago than it is today after a few years of heavy pounding by big, weighty machines instead of horses.

"Certainly I owe my present age of eighty-plus," said the survivor, "to that lovely soft black soil. And my mother's comments when we got home were as typical of her as were my brother's. 'You must be in the Covenant and should live a long time if your luck holds.' And I'm keeping my fingers crossed!"

Well they say it's better to be born lucky than rich and I don't suppose there are that many people alive at over eighty who can remember an iron roller going over them at the age of seven.

I stop to look at a pile of bog-oaks that have been dug up out of the fen, black and hard as coal. They'd keep Mr Dow busy. Nearby is a large patch of comfrey, the healing-herb; a plant that has been used in herbal medicine for two thousand years. The Greeks and the Romans used it and it has been used by herbalists in this country since the fifteenth century. Its leaves can be dried and crushed and used for making tea, a mild, pale beverage which is quite soothing and refreshing with a slice of lemon.

*   *   *

Another man I meet unexpectedly today is also a solitary man, an individual who prefers to live his own life rather than surrender to the conveyor-belt. His name is Geoffrey Armstrong and he is an artist, working alone in his barn out in the Cambridgeshire fens, making art out of things from the earth, mainly large, impressive wood sculptures from the remains of old trees that once drew their strength from the black soil thousands of years ago.

Geoffrey was born in South Africa in 1945 but now lives with his English wife and family in her native corner of the fens. He's not an easy man to find and I go down droves I have not travelled since a boy. I find him, locked away in his barn on the edge of those vast fields, in silence and isolation, shielded even from the scenes outside by sheets of polythene over the windows.

How then did he first respond to this landscape?

" I took to it straightaway, I think. The light was different, the cycle of the year was different, the climate was different and, in some ways, the material was different. And yet I was able to accept all this because I knew it had to be part of me."

" What about the flatness?"

" No, that didn't surprise me or impress me all that much. I'd been used to flat landscapes, but on a much bigger scale of course. It was the atmosphere. There was a kind of primitive quality about the place that excited me. I felt I could get back to the basic conflicts in nature, to the source of true creative energy, if you like. Here, the elements seemed nearer . . . As you can see, I don't set out to create works of art that are visually meant to represent any aspect of this fen landscape as such. These sculptures that you see here are not symbolic of anything I see out there; not images of the natural world as I see it. All I'm trying to do is to find out what is in the piece of wood in the first place. It's the wood that matters, not me. *We* can't create, only reveal it."

" I can see what you mean, but working out here, not only with these materials but surrounded also by all these fields, must mean something to you, or have some influence?"

" Oh yes, I'm sure it does. Our environment, wherever we are, is important and does something for us. This fen landscape has some influence on me as a person, but I don't feel that I belong to it in the sense that you do. My roots are not here. My roots are still in South Africa. But does that matter? We take part of the landscape with us wherever we go because each landscape adds something to us—or should. For instance, I would like to work in an industrial landscape for a change, using steel instead of wood, but that does not mean to say that I would necessarily forget this landscape or prefer the other. I would just be applying myself to a different light, a different environment, and to different materials. After all, it all comes out of the same earth. At the moment I live and work in the fens because it's where my home is, but *my* world is here, in this barn, with the wood and the stone. I am trying to find the pattern of life, the energy, conflict, birth and life-force, if you like, that once existed in the trees. I am a craftsman coming to terms with something that has its own identity and form; something that has been around a lot longer than you or me. It's easier to do that out here because I like the silence. I like the space around me. Perhaps I brought something of my own native landscape with me, in fact I'm sure I did, but that has now merged into what I feel about the fens. I love it out here, I really do!"

I walk around his workshop looking at the huge pieces of wood that have been carved and polished into new life—the elm, walnut, pear, oak and ash. Geoffrey Armstrong works on a large scale, perhaps because the landscape is on a large scale and perhaps because the trees themselves were bigger than man.

" True, I can't reduce things. I can't work in miniature, at least not with wood for that would be depriving it of a natural power and force inherent within it. We can't bring nature down to our level, we can only try to release it and to understand what has been going on for thousands of years. I can't impose my interpretations on the material, that's why I don't want to paint the fens as such, or recreate in wood any physical likeness of what I see outside this barn. I suppose when the wind's howling, when it's snowing or when the sun is beating down and the harvest is being gathered in, then it also has something to do with what's going on here, in my workshop. It's all part of the pattern. I'm trying to make things live again and you are trying to make things live again. That, surely, is what being an artist means—giving life!"

Looking around this barn I have had the feeling more than once that I have walked into a strange kind of primeval forest; and yet, within the shaped and polished works of art, I am seeing for the first time both the cruelty and the dignity of nature; death as a source of life; art as a means of preservation, or transformation. I find myself looking at a new dimension of the familiar fen landscape, a new pattern in my native country. The wood and the earth, the chisel and the plough, the silence and the winds; man and nature.

I find myself struck by the intensity of this particular man's vision, by the way in which he has accepted the responsibility of an artist to be honest with himself and serious about his art, even if no one wants to know. The loneliness, the frustration, the lack of success are, understandably, difficult aspects of life to live with for we are all human and occasionally need to have our faith restored. But Geoffrey Armstrong is, I'm sure, first and foremost an artist making art out of nature, not a trinket-maker for coffee-tables; not even a very good salesman of his work.

" I feel I must spend my energy here, not in the Market Place, and if I have to go potato-picking now and again, so be it. At least I know I shall have done my best here. If I have to go back to South Africa to sell my work, then I know I shall be taking something of this land with me."

The roots of trees, the deformed branches, the thorns and stones around me have somehow taken on a new kind of life as I stand here, as if, any moment, they might breathe or groan or slouch away like some mythological creatures into the pre-historic swamps and forests of the ancient fens before man came to cultivate and govern. They have a raw majesty.

When I step out of the barn into the overcast day the natural landscape has an even stranger impact on me. Somehow the phantom mists have dispersed. The long, low, black fields stretch into the distant forest of clouds. I smell the dust on a clump of nettles. The past and the present are as one. The well-farmed fields are here, but only just. Underneath you sense that the earth has been tamed only temporarily. Somewhere out there is a power we have not conquered, and perhaps never will. In the end we are the subjects being moulded, fashioned, carved, stripped to the bone. We look at the world through other eyes and learn to wonder why we took it all so much for granted.

I shut the barn door and leave the artist to get on with his work. I've no idea of the time and do not want to look at my watch. In the distance I can see a town, a church spire—but why hurry back to the familiar, to the present?

I pick up a book of Anglo-Saxon poems I have with me in the car and by the deserted roadside I read

A man who on these walls wisely looked
Who sounded deeply this dark life
Would think back to the blood spilt here,

Weigh it in his wit. His word would be this:
Where is that horse now? Where are those men?
Where is the hoard-sharer?
Where is the house of the feast? Where the hall's uproar?

Alas, bright cup! Alas, burnished fighter!
Alas, proud prince! How that time has passed,
Dark under night's helm, as though it had never been.

*　　*　　*

Prehistoric, Anglo-Saxon, nineteenth century, artists and horse-keepers, barns, cottages and ruined mead-halls. What a day it has been!

I drive home on roads that will be deserted now until the morning. A barn-owl swoops low and ghostly in front of me, disappearing behind a knot of willow trees.

After supper I still feel restless; not discontented but anxious to get even more out of such a generous day. I walk out of the precincts to watch the sun setting beyond what is, at the moment, a half-demolished city. The broken buildings, the iron railway bridge and factory chimneys suddenly become beautiful in the fiery light. The effect of the sunset is not only on the western horizon but over the whole sky. Smoked-salmon pink clouds are draped like royal awnings overhead. Green, blue, mauve and purple ribbons are woven into them and the eastern horizon deepens to a wood-pigeon grey. The sun itself cannot be seen but scatters its gifts liberally from a crimson dais. The brilliance is too much for the eyes and I am blind to the material things nearby. When I close my eyes they are filled with a burning blackness.

On such a showing it is possible to believe that the sun is losing 4 million tons a second, which is, so I'm told, " 240 million tons a minute, which is 650 times the rate at which water is pouring over Niagara ".

But why spoil a good sunset with scientific explanations! The sun will still be there in the morning, I hope, because I have also read that although it has been losing weight like this daily for 3,000 million years, its total loss still only represents " one part in five thousand of its total mass ".

The colours fade, as if annoyed at my thoughts, and I walk

back into the calmness of the precincts which are now in shadow. It's still too early to go indoors and the warm evening is too good to lose.

I walk round the eastern end of the cathedral where those faceless figures of a past civilization look down at us from their crumbling pedestals; twelve wise old men in stone, whose features have been so sharpened by the wind and the rain they look bird-like, ancient Egyptian, all knowing. But eyeless, they are not dumb. Bone-cramped with sitting, their hands are not utterly meaningless. Stones teach in the same way that the stars do, or the sea, or the sun, or the memories of old people.

The stone figures lure me back again into the past and I walk beyond the cathedral and monastic cloisters into Fengate and out to the fields on the edge of town. This is an area where very important archaeological work has been done in recent years, particularly by Francis Pryor, whose book *People of the Dawn* tells the exciting story of the earliest settlers in this part of England from as far back as 3000 B.C.

To stand alone near one of these sites, on such an evening as this, is to feel that strange mixture of insignificance and achievement. You can look back over five thousand years and tell yourself that we have, after all, accomplished much that has blessed civilization. You can also remember that five thousand years is, in fact, a very, very short time and that many civilizations, empires and nations have come and gone in that time.

But again, why trouble myself with such thoughts? With the mist rising evocatively from the fields and the stars beginning to appear in the summer night's late sky such questions do not stay in the mind too long. I wouldn't want to change places with anyone of five thousand years ago or with anyone in five thousand years to come. It is enough to survive in our own time. The sea, the fields, the sun and the stars will be there for others. If we do not understand too much about them, do they know any better about us?

> How little the stars know
> as they move each night
> over the earth.
> How little they know
> of our fragile worlds,
> of what can happen

between two darknesses.
Each moment on the sky
moves constellations
slowly towards their place
in heaven's calendar
and yet, between each move,
between one night and the next
when movement is not seen,
our worlds collapse,
love changes course,
tears leave the body dry.
And then the heart—
how little the stars know
of the human heart.
Before they move one
nerve-end on Time's face,
before they stir one limb
across the sky, our hearts
tread continents of pain,
our lives change overnight.
Who would have thought
So much could happen
in a star's breath?

*   *   *

When I walk back to the house my mind is still full of the day's events and my head rings with phrases it is hard to forget.

"Jack was a horse-keeper I knew, ever so gentle, a lovely man with horses."

"Call again, any time you like."

"A terrible waste, boys and horses."

"It's the longest week I've ever known."

"We can't bring nature down to our level, we can only try to release it."

"How lovely are Thy dwellings."

How lovely indeed.

7

Some Kind of Gratitude

It's almost too good to be true; too good to last. The sky today has a blueness that reminds me of the blue-bag my mother used to put in the dolly-tub on wash-days when I was a child. My 'Monday-morning-blues' never were—and seldom are—grey, weary depressions or feelings of 'here-we-go-again'. They are bright, optimistic mornings of newness, fresh beginnings and soap-sud sweetness. In fact the last four Mondays have been extremely good ones.

* * *

That memory of those long-ago wash-days takes my mind back to summers I thought I'd forgotten all about, to a time when summers were sweet with the dust on nettles and fallen apples, when small, ordinary worlds became new kingdoms in them-selves.

Most of us, I would think, have some recollection of a certain part of the house or garden that is, or was, specially ours. For me it was the old wash-house at the bottom of the garden, a broken-down building of many-coloured bricks and ill-fitting roof-tiles that allowed peep-holes to the sky. It was a place of secrets and fears, joy and sadness. It was where I could go to spill guilty tears after getting into trouble and it was where, on many occasions, those wild, uninhibited dreams of childhood were born.

I recall it now with all its smells, glows, heaves and broods of summer. It was so many things apart from a wash-house. It was where we also kept the coal, where father chopped the kindling for our fires and kept his bicycle, and where grandfather plucked the latest victim from the chicken-run, his bony hands creating a snowstorm of feathers that whirled in a downy blizzard round his head as he prepared the bird for our Sunday table.

It was also, as its name implies, the place where my mother did the weekly wash, performing in a grotto of steam (and with the help of that dolly-tub) the Monday miracle of making our grimy clothes clean, where the sheets and shirts were hauled from a boiling cauldron of soap-suds, white and timid as rain-drenched ghosts.

We had a fire in the wash-house on Saturday nights too when the water was boiled for our weekly bath. We didn't bath in the wash-house because it was about a hundred yards from the house. The water was carried in pails up to our tiny kitchen where a long zinc bath stood, like a ship in dry dock, waiting to receive both water and child. The boiling water was cooled with cold rain-water from the butt outside the door. Then in I went, to be hauled out a few minutes later, white and laundered for another week.

The wireless was also part of those summer Saturday-night rituals and I still associate ' In Town Tonight ', ' Variety Music Hall ', Vic Oliver, Jack Warner, or Old Mother Riley and Kitty with bath-night. Looking at the fretworked sunrays of that magic speaker from which all those sounds came I was puzzled as to how, week after week, the same voices, music, laughter and comedians travelled through the air and then got caught up in our wireless aerial to emerge in our room with all the familiarity of favourite uncles. There was no greater sense of danger then as a child than to creep up to that wireless-set when no one was looking and turn one of those brown knobs that immediately flung all the voices, tangled and incoherent, back into space.

Finally, when the rest of the family had finished bathing, the old zinc battleship was hung once more on the wall outside until next Saturday night came round again.

From the small square window of my bedroom I watched the smoke fade from the wash-house chimney and the first faint stars appear over the roof-tops of the town.

Summer was born in that wash-house. It was where the seeds were sorted out for the garden, the potatoes had been encouraged to chit ready for planting, where the rake and hoe were taken from their hooks ready for use. It was where the cat had her kittens, where the straw for my rabbits was kept and where, from beneath a dusty pile of sacks, I usually found my cricket-bat or whip-and-top, and where eventually we had to look for our buckets and spades as the summer holidays approached.

Despite the hardships of the ' thirties ' we always managed a week's holiday at somewhere like Heacham, Hunstanton or Skegness, and I can see some of those boarding-houses now as vividly as I can remember the wash-house. Walking into the house we had chosen, I would gaze timidly at its size and worry about the prospects of keeping up my best behaviour for so long among strangers. The steep, straight stairs led to a mysterious landing of several doors. Which one was ours? Whose were the others? The hall was covered with heavy wallpaper patterned with roses, the barometer had a notice underneath which said ' DO NOT TAP ', and the antler hat-stand held walking-sticks, umbrellas and a butterfly-net. And then into the bedroom with its towering wardrobe and marbled wash-basin, and that peculiar boarding-house smell that seemed to be a mixture of all the smells of the human-beings that had ever stayed there. From the window I looked out expecting the sea to be lapping at the garden gate. It was usually in the distance, glimpsed between roof-tops and a good ten-minute walk after breakfast. But it was worth it. The smell of the sea cleared my head of every other smell and as I ran down on to the beach I whacked at the dazzling sunlight with my spade.

Here was a world of castles, donkeys, starfish, cockles, ice-creams and doughnuts. Clowns played on the pier, elephants paraded through the streets, men took our photographs as we walked along or offered to clean our shoes, and a blind man made wonderful sculptures out of sand. Shells had the secret of locking the roar of the sea in their spiral shapes and the waves brought in bottles with invisible messages. Tiny crabs lay like precious brooches in rock pools and jelly-fish fouled the sand like huge gobs of spit. It was like the creation all over again. To disturb one strand of primeval seaweed was to reveal the beginnings of Time.

I returned to one of those holiday resorts just a few weeks ago. Not so much has changed and yet everything's different. It is difficult for me now to see that world with the eyes of a child experiencing that world. The bathing costumes are different of course and so too are some of the saucy postcards. The nylon deckchairs, windbreaks, picnic-baskets and transistor-radios are different, but the children appear to be enjoying the same things—making sandcastles, looking for shells, watching a Punch and Judy show, riding a moth-eaten donkey, and licking ice-creams. I didn't see any beach-time talent competitions or shoe-shine boys. The pier was closed and it was difficult to buy anything under 20p. But the sea was there, and the sun and the sand. A warm wind blew off the cliffs and a child was flying his kite. For a moment I wondered how he'd 'escaped out' and gone back to live his summers again.

*   *   *

How easily the mind can be seduced into a pleasant nostalgia all because a patch of blue sky reminds you of a long-ago wash-day. Does today's sky still live up to that vivid Reckitt's blue memory? Yes, it's as blue now as it was then and I am tempted once more into the open spaces. I might go as far as Norfolk, perhaps to Hunstanton or just to King's Lynn—I've no plans. I'm grateful I have the choice to follow my nose and trust the smells in the air. It's a day for sauntering and, as Henry David Thoreau said, "To saunter is an art." You have to follow where your instincts lead. The adventure is the unexpected.

I set off vaguely into Cambridgeshire first because, more than anything, I want quiet roads. I drive towards the Bedford Middle Level, Benwick, Doddington, Manea and Welney.

The water of the River Nene is glass calm again as I leave the city. The cattle and pylons are reflected so perfectly you could turn the scene upside down and it would look the same. All the waters in the drains too shine with a summer stillness, as if the warm sun has ironed them free of creases.

I cross Sixteen Foot Drain, a ten-mile-long silver measuring tape that could have been used in *Gulliver's Travels* or *Alice in Wonderland,* so far beyond the limits of acceptability it looks.

All the combine-harvesters are out in force making the most of the good weather. It's always an impressive sight. The last great act of summer. A scene where the gods meet. The year has been building up to this moment. Wherever I look the final ceremony is taking place. The golden fields are changing. Excitement, or fulfilment, is in the air. The vast arena sweats with anticipation. I want to be part of the harvest again, only

an onlooker, but one who can appreciate all that has gone into
its production.

I saunter on until I reach Manea and then the instinct takes
over. I had half decided to turn left to Welney and make my
way along Ten Mile Bank, Denver and Norfolk. But impulsively
I turn right and make my way instead down to Purls Bridge
and Welches Dam on the Old Bedford River.

It's not the best time of the day or year to go bird-watching
but it's a marvellous place to be on such a morning. Here you
become part of the Great Ouse washlands which owe their
existence to Cornelius Vermuyden and his drainage engineers
of the seventeenth century. They still form the largest inland
area of regularly grazed marshland in Britain and are extremely
valuable as a nature reserve for birds which need these solitary
places for their habitat. Every care is taken here to protect the
birds and the washlands, and the Royal Society for the
Protection of Birds must be congratulated again for the way it
has informed the public of the great asset to wildlife. Here the
serious bird-watcher can enjoy nearly 2,000 acres of wild land
and everything has been done to make a day on the marshes a
rewarding one. The paths are well marked, the stiles have a
lift-up bar, the hides themselves are thoughtfully spaced,
comfortable and dry, with informative wall-charts. They have
good names too—Halfway Hide, Stockdale Hide, Osier End
Hide, Cottier Hide, Rickwood and Common Wash Hide. If
you're lucky you can see many species during one watch. The
washlands are well known for pintail, mallard, redshank,
godwits, shovelers, quail, geese and swans. The winter months
especially, when the floods are out, produce some remarkable
spectacles of bird movement, both in variety and numbers. It's
a lonely world in winter and the long roads leading to the
washland have a frightening silence about them. The land will
appear dead. The sky will probably be putty grey. The reeds
brittle with frost. Then snow or fog can so transform this
landscape that you can be lost within minutes. It's as though
these very secret places were trying to repel you, keep you
away, or at least remind you that you are, after all, only human.

But not today. Although the roads are lonely enough they
are also bright, clear and warm. Their power today is mainly
in their impressive length and straightness which once again
seem to defy measurement.

I park the car near Welches Dam and follow the signposts to the hides, keeping to the lower bank path as requested, and not on the top of the bank where I could be seen by birds miles away. Here you are entering a world that has not known anything but the wildness of nature. The very character of the place with its willows, reeds, weeds, teasels and grasses gives you a feeling of walking into some undiscovered country. You feel you are stepping on primitive earth and the silence is watching.

Between the teasels, thistles and sorrel small moths and peacock butterflies float like wind-blown pieces of silk. On my left, as I walk to my chosen hide, are the expansive fens of Langwood, Byall, Wimblington and then Upwell. On my right is the sheltering bank and that vast no-man's-land that stretches into eternity.

I enter into the hide, lift the narrow look-out panel and gasp in amazement. Seeing the fens through this 'letter-box' seems to magnify them. In the middle distance is the bank of the New Bedford River (that historic landmark of Vermuyden's work) and on the horizon is a very clear view of Ely Cathedral.

It's interesting, while waiting for some birds to appear, to speculate on the view of this land the monks would have had from their lantern tower in those days before the fens were drained.

The importance of these two artificial rivers—the Old Bedford and the New—is worth mentioning again because they have been vital to the formation of the fen country as we know it today. The New Bedford River, which was cut in 1650, is the most important and keeps the whole of the upland waters of the Great Ouse out of the Ely loop between Earith and Denver. It also acts in reverse and takes the whole of the tidal waters which enter the Ouse from the Wash laden with silt. If this water was allowed into the original course of the Ouse at high tide it would drown much of the valuable farm land in the South Level. As it is the New Bedford, with its built-in gradient, works as a flush, keeping the fens free of unwanted silt and surplus water. If the tides are high and the rainfalls heavy, then flooding can be allowed on the 5,500 acres which serve as a reservoir between the length of the two Bedford rivers. The land around Ely therefore is well protected and it is unlikely that anyone from the cathedral's lantern tower will ever see quite the same amount of water as the monks did a few hundred years ago.

Before leaving the subject of fen-drainage (for I have dealt more fully with this in *Portrait of the Fen-Country*) I will tell you of an incident in which the tail turned round and bit the dog.

I was showing a party of visitors around the fens one Sunday afternoon and telling them of how Vermuyden had been compelled to import a labour force of a thousand Scottish prisoners-of-war who had been captured by Cromwell's troops. Five hundred notices were distributed throughout the area warning the local people not to help the prisoners to escape. For any who did try to get away it would be " Death without mercy ". The authorities needn't have worried too much about the locals being that friendly for there was certainly no love lost between the fen-tigers and the Scots who were helping to deprive the fen-men of much of the wildfowling and fishing which gave them their livelihood. The locals not only sabotaged the drainage works but frequently took their resentment out on the prisoners. As we looked over one of the nearby fens on that particular Sunday afternoon I decided to add a little spice to the narrative by saying that there was a story that two Scottish soldiers were stabbed to death one night as they guarded the day's work and in the morning their bodies were found in the mud. Their fellow-prisoners, on finding their murdered comrades, vowed that the fen would be haunted evermore by the spirits of these men. I explained to my passengers that although I had never seen the ghosts myself I had heard it said in the village that on certain nights of the year two spectral figures could be seen walking across the washlands. There were a few groans and shivers and then I sat down, instructing our coach-driver to continue with the journey. When we reached Ely, for tea at the Fire-Engine Restaurant, two elderly ladies (who had lived in the fens years ago) came up to me and said, " You know them two Scottish ghosts you were talking about! We've seen 'em! "

Well I didn't know whether I'd accidentally stumbled on a true ghost story or whether my guests were just that much better at ' telling a tall 'un! ' I must admit that it took some of the smugness out of my smile and I kept to facts for the rest of the afternoon excursion.

*   *   *

I do not know how long I've sat in the hide looking out at the ghost-haunted marshes and Ely Cathedral. This is a day that also makes meaningless the measurement of time.

When I do emerge into the fierce brightness of the day I notice that the sun has moved quite some way on its own journey over the sky; it's no good, I still can't get out of the habit of thinking that the earth remains still and the universe revolves around us. It must be something to do with this landscape.

I leave the river-bank of the Old Bedford and decide to go to Welney after all. I then cut back on the other side of the New Bedford towards Pymore so that I can view the washlands from a different angle. The village gardens also celebrate the day with colourful flower-beds and neat lawns. Almost every house has a notice at its gate advertising fruit and vegetables for sale. The prices look a bit on the high side and the word FRESH is underlined as if to justify the few pence above market prices.

From Pymore I go to Downham-in-the-Isle, a very attractive village which earns its awards and still proudly—thank God—blazons forth its true identity with the Isle of Ely, another part of Old England that has, like Huntingdon, the Soke of Peterborough, Rutland and the Ridings of Yorkshire officially disappeared . . . Downham-in-the-Isle has music in its name which isn't heard if you just say Downham, Cambs.

The higher land of the Isle of Ely itself is very noticeable as you drive into Ely, and today the city looks radiantly *alive*. For once it's wise not to be put off by William Cobbett's condemnation of a place and I certainly do not share his views on Ely when he writes, " Ely is what one may call a miserable little town: very prettily situated but poor and mean. Everything seems to be on the decline . . ."

Not today, Mr Cobbett. Perhaps 150 years ago it might have looked like that, but today it looks prosperous and charitable, busy and rich. The market is doing a brisk and noisy trade. The stalls flash with bright colours and the stall-holders gabble and chant their wares. The cathedral is like a pot of honey surrounded by a thousand bees. It's amazing how people swarm to cathedrals and yet don't really care all that much about the functions they perform, treating them very much like stately homes or museums. And I suppose one must be honest and say that a good many cathedrals have gone along with this image and found the tourist trade a lucrative way of paying off death-duties.

Ely's cathedral, however, has to be looked at in wonder for it is something of a miracle when you think of the condition of this countryside at the time the place was built. It was a true 'island' church dominating the Isle itself and the fen waters around it. Its history has been told many times before and there is no need to repeat it here, but it is a building that cannot be ignored on any day of the year and in today's light it looks as if it might have been carved out of alabaster. My own favourite part of the cathedral is the lovely, spacious, clear-light Lady Chapel where you can stand in airy peace. Here again the thoughts are interrupted by that Cromwellian spectre who haunts so much of the fens for the eyes notice that every figure in the chapel is headless. The 'idols' have been systematically disfigured.

But the place to be on a day like this is down by the river, a busy river with people messing about in boats and amateur artists messing about in paints. There's not much to excite the Royal Academy but the painters look relaxed and contented. They may not be doing much for nature but nature is clearly doing a lot for them. One picture in particular, however, does stand out from all the others as much for its subject as for its technique. It's a bare tree trunk by the water's edge in a meadow opposite. I like it and ask the elderly lady why she'd chosen to paint a bare, dead and almost branchless tree in summer. "Because it's there," she says.

Well we all have our Everests I suppose and her reason is as good as any. I like her picture enough to covet it and wish the paint was dry enough for me to run off with it.

I walk back to the quayside and the pub. What a mixture of smells you get from a busy riverside. The water smells of oil and dead fish. The air smells of paint and fish-'n'-chips, of pipe-smoke and cigars, of beer and spirits. It's just like being on holiday at the seaside, only there's no beach, no Punch and Judy Show or saucy postcards. A decorated narrow boat has its wares on display on the roof—coffee-pots, mugs, bowls, frying-pans and jugs. On one of the cabin cruisers someone is playing a guitar and singing to a dog. The gulls protest. The accents, people, sights, and smells excite. The heat of the afternoon wraps them all together into a bouquet and offers them to the nostrils. One deep breath and "Ah!" you say, "time to get back to the country and the open spaces."

I wander back up to the town, discover a second-hand bookshop I'd not found before, buy three or four volumes (including an 1899 publication on Peterborough Cathedral) and then take to the road again.

The land between Ely and Newmarket, Ely and Cambridge, is particularly good harvesting country this year. It hasn't been an easy summer because of the mixed weather and some of the crops have looked very sorry for themselves until this week. But today the sun has made all the difference. The steady drone of machines, the farmers dashing from one field to another to see how their men are getting on. The dust in the air. The growing columns of smoke as they set fire to some of the corn-stubble. And the afternoon slips too quickly for them towards evening.

The low rays of the sun filter through clouds of dust-haze. The unburnt stubble is almost bronze in such a rich light. The uncut fields shine like polished brass. The dyke-sides of wild flowers, reeds and grass glow in the soft air. Patches of purple loosestrife, mallow, red campion, scabious, daisies and poppies, decorate the margins of the fields until the whole landscape becomes an illuminated manuscript, a medieval psalter in praise of the earth.

One by one the combines finish their fields or their day's work and the air becomes very still. I am reminded of a short poem by the Sicilian poet Salvatore Quasimodo

> Everyone is alone on the heart of the earth
> pierced by a ray of sun:
> and suddenly it's evening.

In the quietness of such an evening it is easy to feel again that ancient pull of the earth, to feel the strong links with the past and the early rituals of seed-time and harvest from the beginning. In the distance is a solitary cottage. It could be the first hut man ever built. What invisible or legendary thread holds us to those remote, primitive tremblings? What spirit still beats faintly in the blood? I step on to an unburnt field of stubble and hear ancient voices speaking:

> Before the first field received its corn
> the earth breathed love.

Before the low light of the sun combed
through the sickled straw
the blood beat with love.
Before the flint was fashioned to an axehead
and the grass was turned into a furrow,
Man looked at woman
and the man said "Love!"

And after the dance,
after the usual ceremony,
the straw was plaited into a roof
for Love said "Build me a house
where I might sit and eat."
And the forests were thinned out,
the woods were chopped down,
the leaves were stripped from the branches
and the woman looked at her husband
and his wife said "Love!"

Over the roof-tops the stars waited for naming,
each fixed constellation
on its journey of seasons,
each holding its course for man's destination;
and the night sang of love.
Over the hearthside the mother laboured,
over the rug rocked a warming cradle,
After the summer came the fall of the apple,
and the couple looked at their fruit
and the child said "Love!"

*　　*　　*

The art of sauntering has taken the day. It hasn't been what I expected. My final impressions are certainly a far cry from those early thoughts about wash-houses, childhood and seaside holidays. I didn't get to King's Lynn or Hunstanton this time. Another day perhaps. It's time to go home now.

I turn off towards Soham and drive into Wicken—a village of many happy memories, both in the local and on the fen. Some of the old characters have disappeared over the last few years and their kind will never be replaced. The atmosphere isn't the same without them.

The atmosphere of Wicken Fen itself, however, does not change all that much, at least not in the same way. It has its moods but it can always be relied upon to come up with something. As usual with these reserves in the fens you are aware of a remarkable stillness as you enter them and, with the stillness, there is that marvellous awareness of smells. You get it at Woodwalton and you get it at Wicken. They're different, but unforgettable. I remember one summer day on Wicken when, in the sultry heat, the scent of the flowers made you feel you were walking through the dark caverns of an ancient wine-cellar where the suns and fruits of other summers had been stored away for years and today was tasting day.

Wicken, Stretham, Haddenham and Earith; magical names at the end of any day or time of the year, but more so today.

Westwards the pomegranate sun is bruised and crimson, fading quickly on a smoky sky. And suddenly it's night.

Ramsey, Whittlesey, Peterborough and home. I feel as if a whole year has passed since I left these precincts this morning.

Trying to put these recollections into some kind of order the day says what the roads, the rivers and fields have already said: "We are here to defy measurement."

True, you cannot pin days like this into a calendar or encase them in a diary. They do not belong to our concept of time or space. All they ask is that we be grateful.

No one at the moment could be more grateful. I have pictures in my mind that night cannot dim. But I say to the stars at the end of this day: "There are some kinds of gratitude that cannot be measured." We can but sigh like contented dogs and sleep, hoping a sigh is eloquent enough to give thanks.

8

By the Waters of the Welland

I have deserted Cambridgeshire today and gone back to south
Lincolnshire to spend a few hours by our third major fenland
river—the Welland.

Like the Great Ouse and the Nene it also has at least two
very different characters—its winding, natural course through
stone villages and rich grazing-land, and its more austere,
turgid, down-to-earth rôle through the Lincolnshire fens into
its outfall in the Wash. There, in those sulky waters roughened
by a north-east wind, the three rivers mingle, come together
like weary travellers and compare notes.

From Market Harborough to Stamford the Welland is as
attractive as any river could be, flowing gently through
farmlands and stone villages bright and warm as crystallized
ginger—Rockingham, Thorpe-by-Water, Wakerley and Dud-
dington. What river would not be proud to have such delightful
places on its banks. Rivers are so good at planning the positions
and shapes of villages and the Welland has done it exceptionally
well. It moves through this landscape with the grace and
dignity of a queen acknowledging her subjects, indulging a
little in the scenery that it knows it will not enjoy much beyond
Stamford.

At Stamford it has to compete with a town that has many
attractions, a town praised by writers, painters and architects
for generations. Sir Walter Scott admired Stamford, so did
Turner, and so did Cobbett—not the easiest man to please. In
the spring of 1830 he was able to write: " I went to Stamford
and in the evening spoke to about 200 farmers and others, in a
large room in a very fine and excellent inn called Standwell's
Hotel, which is, with few exceptions, the nicest inn that I have
ever been in . . ." He also found that the town was pleasantly set
" in country of rich arable land and grass fields, and of

beautiful meadows ". He liked many of the stone houses and was equally impressed by " the large, lofty churches " except where they had been spoilt, damaged and defaced " by the ungrateful Protestant barbarians!"

That's one thing about Cobbett, he never pulls his punches. He's a splendidly entertaining writer to read because of his own passion for his own causes, for his intolerant condemnation of others whose views he does not share, and his remarkable command of the English language. His fiery pen can still shock, enrage, provoke and win applause. William Hazlitt wrote of him: " He is not only unquestionably the most powerful political writer of the day, but one of the best writers in the language. He speaks and thinks plain, broad, downright English . . ."

Cobbett's *Rural Rides* is still a classic of observation, comment and descriptive writing, but equally fascinating is *The Autobiography of William Cobbett*, with the sub-title ' The Progress of a Plough-boy to a seat in Parliament '.

Anyway, Cobbett liked Stamford and clearly had a very good inn for the night as well as a good audience for his speech.

Stamford's fame and history is long and unbroken. It has not suffered the transfiguration that many of our old towns have in trying to fit into the twentieth century. Cobbett would still find fine houses, lofty churches and beautiful meadows.

The Saxons also thought it was a good place to be and developed it into a town of some importance until the Danish invasion destroyed most of what had been established. Daniel Defoe tells us that " it was burnt by the Danes about 1500 years ago, it then being a flourishing city ".

In medieval times the town was celebrated throughout Europe as a centre of religious learning and there are still signs of the many monastic buildings that once stood within its walls. Blackfriars, Whitefriars, Greyfriars and Austin Friars all had communities in Stamford and at one time it looked as if it would become the alternative university town to Oxford when the rebellious students there transferred to some of the local schools. At the request of the authorities, however, they were ordered by Edward III to return to the original colleges in Oxford, leaving those students who'd gone to Cambridge to establish their adopted city as the major alternative seat of learning in the country.

There is, as it happens, a link between Stamford and Cambridge, for Lady Margaret Beaufort—who lived at Colly-weston three miles away, and who was the mother of Henry VII—founded the local Guild of St Catherine, and St John's College, Cambridge.

The number of monarchs who have been entertained in Stamford is impressive even when read quickly. I won't list them individually, but between William I and Elizabeth II at least sixteen reigning monarchs have been officially received in the town, not to mention the scores of royal relatives who have accompanied them. The great house of Burghley nearby has always been an added attraction and has increased its popularity by providing such an historic setting for its horse trials.

The Civil War did not ignore Stamford either. Although Royalist at heart the townspeople found themselves living in a Parliamentarian stronghold. Cromwell was here, of course. Charles I came too, disguised as a servant, in 1646, but was betrayed and so spent his last night as a free man, on Stamford soil. And you could go on finding an unbroken chain of important events and people that have kept Stamford alive.

But Stamford is much more than a roll-call of kings. It would still have been a beautiful town if no crowned head had ever slept there or looked upon its streets. It has had an influence, not only scholastically and ecclesiastically, but also commercially. It was famous for its wool as early as A.D. 800, and from 1200 on, this was its premier industry. Continental weavers came over in the sixteenth century and settled here, and its wares were sought after throughout Europe.

Fairs and markets have always been part of Stamford life too and both can still be seen adding colour and congestion to the streets. Good inns and ale, good food and wares, traditions and contemporary events, all make this town on the banks of the Welland an exciting place to explore before going off into the sparser fens of Lincolnshire.

Stamford does not, however, have quite the last word because there are still one or two stone villages and at least one more town that can claim attention before the Welland waters finally disperse into the Wash.

Market Deeping, and the cluster of smaller Deepings around it, provides a gateway to the Lincolnshire fens, though I have to admit I have a preference for entering this landscape from

Crowland and Deeping High Bank. From here you get such a wide expanse of low country spread out before you that you can plan almost your whole day from one position.

Stowgate, Deeping St Nicholas, Deeping Common and farms as far as the eye can see, all are busy with their harvests. The land looks good today, shining pale and golden under a cloudless sky. Quite a lot of the crops are already in and soon the fields of Lincolnshire will, like those of Cambridgeshire, be charred and bare until the plough turns them over for winter. Bales of straw stand like a smaller Stonehenge.

I pull a couple of ears of corn, rub them in my hands, blow away the chaff, then nibble the dry, warm and sweet grain. It takes my mind back again to the summers of my childhood when I went out gleaning with my mother. Even after the harvest you could still fill a sack in no time and the memory of the straw-dust stays with me still.

It's not only corn-harvesting going on in these fields today. They have also started lifting the potatoes and in one or two fields gangs of women are laying out the onions for drying. Only the sugar-beet crops are left untouched, waiting for their own time, adding a little more weight, absorbing the last few weeks of summer sun.

Beyond the fields the distance stretches away into an incredible clarity of light. The horizon is a very long way away and yet there is a sharpness in the atmosphere that makes trees and buildings visible miles off.

The midday sky becomes forget-me-not blue, the earth dry-sherry gold. You only need these two colours today to paint this landscape. There are few verticals or buildings to get into perspective. I feel it's something I could almost do myself, but I know the magic would be missing.

I find myself nearly hypnotized by the combines' slow unweaving of the fields—old grandmotherly hands patiently unpicking a woollen shawl that is no longer needed. The earth is shorn for winter.

Once the Welland gets past the Deepings it loses its natural, lazy, ambling course and conforms more to the laws of man. It is no longer the planner, but the planned. Its waters no longer flow under the famous triangular, or Trinity, bridge at Crowland, but from its banks you can look over towards the ancient ruins of the abbey.

Crowland, or Croyland, Abbey is always worth a diversion from any route or arrangements, and I cannot follow the waters of the Welland without pausing again for a few moments. I know I have written a few hundred words about it in previous books but I find there is always something new to say about it, and it is one of my favourite places.

On a warm summer's day there is a deep feeling of peace. Bees hum in and out of the stone walls; a faint vibration of insects comes from the grass. The ruins of the abbey browse through their own history, and you can feel something of the abbey's tradition for healing and learning. You can also feel something of the destruction, especially by the Danes in the ninth century. The abbey here once had a splendid library of illuminated manuscripts, theological works and beautifully illustrated psalters, but like many other monastic treasures these precious books went up in flames and the evidence of men's art and thought were lost.

One of its early benefactors, in the rebuilding of the abbey after the Danish invaders, was Earl Waltheof who was, you will remember, referred to several times when I was writing earlier about Fotheringhay and Sawtry. After Waltheof had been executed, William I gave permission for his body to be moved to Croyland Abbey for burial and it was not long before pilgrims began visiting his tomb, believing him to be a very good and saintly man. This started an ecclesiastical controversy and some twelve years later Waltheof's coffin was opened. Inside lay the completely uncorrupted, undecayed, unblemished body of the earl and, what is more, his head (which had been chopped off) was reunited to the rest of him, with no more than a thin red scar to show where the executioner's blade had struck.

The Abbot Geoffrey, responsible for this extraordinary revelation, is said to have received a vision of Waltheof, with Saint Bartholomew and Saint Guthlac reciting in hexameters the saga of the miracle.

Now I ask you, how can you *not* leave the waters of the Welland to visit a place like Croyland Abbey when such deeds and miracles have been seen to be done. You might also be able to touch the skull of the Abbot Theodore (who was slain at the altar by the Danes), if the glass case is still suffering from the damage inflicted upon it by present-day vandals.

I leave Crowland and rejoin the banks of the Welland as it flows nearer to the end of its journey. The last place of any great significance on its route now is Spalding, a town famous today for its bulb industry, its tulip parades, its farming and sugar-beet. It's a lively place and perhaps more aware of belonging to the twentieth century than some of its neighbours. But it too has its roots in the past and there is at least one surviving society very much worthy of mention: The Spalding Gentlemen's Society, founded in 1710 by Maurice Johnson, a lawyer and antiquarian. Its members have included such distinguished men as Sir Isaac Newton, Alexander Pope, John Gay, Joseph Addison and Sir Hans Sloane. Meetings are still held regularly from September to March and the Society preserves the long tradition of inviting eminent speakers to talk on a wide range of subjects—scientific, historic, literary and geographical. I send it birthday greetings for its 300th birthday in forty years' time.

* * *

Between the Welland and the Nene is a landscape that has a character all its own. Here it is still possible to have the roads all to yourself, even in summer, and feel a solitariness that is as healing as any abbey or sacred relic. In summer a heat-haze blurs the horizon. This is land reclaimed from the sea and somehow the sea will never let you forget it. There is a very real water-colour quality about the place. You are not quite sure whether you belong to earth, sky or sea. The only thing you are certain of is that you are surrounded by an amazing amount of space.

The sea is now a long way off beyond the mud-flats of the Wash. The sky is a long way off beyond the high-circling gulls. The land is a long way off beyond the grass verge at the other end of a field. It's between you and nature here—and nature is very, very imposing, very impressive and confident. It momentarily raises an eyebrow at man's threescore years and ten, and returns to its timeless brooding; a prehistoric ghost stirring in its sleep.

It's good to come back to these marshes on a day like this and there is something pleasant in being made to take your time in arriving. After Spalding I go to Holbeach and then the several villages named after it—Holbeach St Matthew, Holbeach St Mark, Holbeach Hurn. You feel the signposts are teasing you, as they do at Whaplode Drove, trying to put you off finding that edge of the world.

It's not an irritating cat-and-mouse game for this is lovely low country to drive through. All the villages, farms, houses and gardens are tidily kept, with considerable personal pride taken in each plot of land. Hedges are neatly trimmed, fields are cared for and there is a quiet feeling of orderliness, even competition, about the whole area. Landowners and tenants are generous with their displays of flowers, and most of the crops look as if they've been prepared specially for exhibition. The long, lonely roads are a pleasure to drive on and a hundred-and-one things attract the attention.

Just ahead of me rabbits are playing hopscotch in the middle of the road and do not want to be disturbed. I slow down to watch them for a few minutes, but however slow you want to go there is some strange power or hunger inside you forcing you to hurry the last mile. The sea calls. The colossal sky beckons.

The sea-wall is the last barrier. You climb on to it breathlessly and the view leaves you with your mouth wide open and your eyes unable for the moment to take in such an expanse. The blue desert of sky is enormous. Little oases of cloud can be seen to the north, but looking east there is nothing but this vast Sahara of blue. To the left I can see the prominent tower of Boston Stump. To the right are King's Lynn, Hunstanton and the Norfolk coastline. Slowly the eyes begin to encompass an aspect of twenty-five miles.

And then you become aware of the stillness, the beautiful quietness of a summer's day in an almost primeval landscape; not silence, because the sweet, humming wind can be heard combing the grass. Today there are no jet-planes screaming low over the marsh, not even skylarks. The peace is unbelievable. Soak it up, drink it, breath it, absorb it into every cell of your body; it may have to last a long time.

The brown, oozy creeks shine in the afternoon sunlight. The royal-blue pencil-line of the sea's horizon grows more intense, more vivid. The tide turns. The wind is suddenly fresher. The sea-birds become active—gulls, terns, dunlin and oyster-catchers. The oystercatchers particularly make their presence felt and I read somewhere that in Scandinavian countries they are called 'scolders'—most appropriate!

Then there's the smell, that magical smell of sea-borne breezes blowing in off the marshes, pure, clear, invigorating and virgin. You imagine that this is how all the earth's air must have smelt in the very beginning, millions of years ago, at the time of Eden.

I stand for a long time looking out to sea, looking up into that vivid blueness, feeling so much part of this unique country.

The creeks begin to fill with water. The mud is covered. The footprints are washed away. The pencil-line of sea has now broadened into a more positive brush-stroke. Close your eyes and you lose your own identity for a moment as you become part of this rare atmosphere.

I have spent many contented hours on these unspoilt acres but few have been happier than today's. The visit here today has been perfect. It will belong to that special collection of summer memories that will be talked about in years to come. I shall probably be like old Timothy Scarlett telling tales round an inn's hearth one winter evening and I shall say " I once knew a summer day so much like paradise that I doubt if any gathered here will ever know such a day in your lifetimes." I shall be like the old man I refer to in my Introduction, today will defy all records, official reports or statistics. It will be a good day, because I say so. For once I can share the sentiments of Rupert Brooke writing about a different sea:

> Today I have been happy. All the day
> I held the memory of you, and wove
> Its laughter with the dancing light o' the spray.

*　　*　　*

I drive back along equally deserted roads. The sun is already drifting slowly towards the western horizon. My face is warm and fresh from the air on the marsh. There is a reluctance to reach civilization too soon. I can still feel the gentle sway of water, the ageless rhythm of the sea, the penetrating blueness of the afternoon sky. I have been recharged. Something of the ancient spirit has returned to me. I think of something that Keats said: " I am certain of nothing but the holiness of the heart's affection and the truth of the imagination."

Far off, inland, smoke rises from burning corn-stubble. From this mysterious and deserted corner of England, with the North Sea behind you, it does not need much imagination to be back in the ninth century, to see again that dark, swelling cloud in the sky as the smoke rising from the ravaged ruins of Spalding, Thorney or Croyland. There is a shiver of movement in the reeds. A little panic of wind moves through the grass. The light fails but the air does not lose its warmth. In the villages old people are still sitting outside their open doors, holding on to the last moments of day. Some talk, some smoke, some crouch on their wooden chairs and just stare at the ground in front of them. A group of children are playing at the corner of the street. They belong to a different world.

Soon the lights of the city begin to shine more clearly. The countryside behind me is now like a giant shadow that disappears when the sun goes in. As I enter the streets of automatic lights and neon signs I am able to say to myself: " I too have belonged to a different world today." All I want to do now is sit in my room, be silent and remember.

Of this much I'm sure: you can pack a whole summer into one day, and it can never leave you.

*   *   *

There is a full moon now shining above the cathedral. The sky is a silvery-grey silk, pinned with small stars. The stones are almost transparent, unreal, shell-like; something risen from the sea, new and fragile. For once the mighty west front takes second place. It is dwarfed tonight by a greater majesty and by something more permanent.

The night is very still; quieter than dew-fall or cobweb making; quieter than snail track or moth flight. Slowly the moon moves behind the tower and spirelets until it is directly behind the needle-spire on the south corner. And now something eerie and magical takes place. This particular spire is undergoing repairs after being struck by lightning and there is a slender ladder reaching to the cross at the top. In the moonlight this ladder looks very frail and narrow outlined against the night space. It becomes more than just a set of rungs waiting for a stonemason or steeplejack. It is Jacob's ladder stretched between earth and heaven. Any moment now someone, something, is going to ascend or descend it—an angel, or Quasimodo; a miracle or revelation; or perhaps the ghosts of that tormented "olive-coloured" lover and his rejected queen.

The moon waits. I wait, certain that "on such a night as this" the eyes will witness sights unseen before. It's worth the watching if only to see the building in this haunting atmosphere. How many of this room's previous tenants saw it so, I wonder?

Moon and stone. The two solids are, at this moment, as bright as water and as light as air. They need each other to make a night of such magic as this—all earthly things forgotten under an enchanting sky. It is a scene no other season could create. Time and place; design and chance. All coming together for just a few moments once a year.

Although the moon moves away from the spire, and the web-like ladder fades in its shadow, the silence remains. It lasts for nearly another hour and then the clock strikes eleven, each note falling like a petal on to still water.

The night air is warm. It flows through my open window with a scent of lime trees and grass. The precincts' cat pads along a wall and slouches off into the dark without a thought for the hour's enchantment, as silent as the waters of the Welland that slink now into the shadows of the Wash.

9
A Pilgrimage to Norfolk

The clouds are on holiday and bask in a deckchair of sky, just gazing at the earth or having forty winks. They've hardly moved all day and, if they have, it has been only to heave with contentment or to turn their faces to the sun. White, fat and harmless, they are like friendly, overweight aunts unashamed of their generous flesh exposed on a summer beach. The horizon is the right place for them to be today, leaving the rest of the sky a swimming-pool blue and as deep as the sea.

The air is filled with warmth and ripe, drowsy colours; with the scent of roses and juicy grass. Roses grow abundantly in the fens, not just in gardens but in fields where the rose-growers cultivate roses as crops, in acres and for profit; thousands of bushes and trees illuminating the countryside with strips of sensational red, orange, yellow and pink.

You surrender yourself wholly to the earth today because you know there is nothing better you can do than become the beneficiary of such a benevolent giver. There may not be another day like it all year. It may well become a day to enlarge upon in years to come, saying " I remember one year we had a summer when there wasn't a cloud in the sky and the sun shone sixteen hours a day and everybody ate out of doors and just let the world get on with it . . ."

Every generation has a recollection like that, and travelling now over Hilgay Fen I know that my mind is taking pictures that will go into the memory's album for an age when the sun may not be shining or I shall not be able to ride over this big, wide, spacious and clear country.

The expanse of land out here today is awesome, even to someone familiar with the fens. Look in any direction and you have an almost defiant flatness that seems to deny the earth its natural curve. The light on such a day once more stretches your vision over distances which you would not have thought possible. As you gaze out over Hilgay Fen and the Southery Fens you are looking at a landscape unique in Britain—and I use that word 'unique' deliberately. There may be other flat landscapes in this country but none quite like this. It is difficult to describe it, or paint it, or photograph it—you can only *see* it in all its magnitude. When I make this comment to a local farmer he casts a brief but knowing eye over the scene and says, " Ah, there's a lot on it!"

This remarkable expanse of farmland is all round you as you continue your journey along Ten Mile Bank towards Denver. As you pause to admire the several thousand acres of fertile country on your left it is worth remembering that several million gallons of water are travelling parallel with you *above* the level of your head. The reason why you can safely use this road now is, as I have suggested elsewhere, a saga in itself. The phrase ' fen drainage ' is too dull to describe its long drama.

Denver is the great meeting place for many waters. Here the Great Ouse sweeps round to collect the water of the River Wissey and then, at the mighty Denver Sluice, joins up with both the Old and New Bedford Rivers, and also the New Relief Channel—all flowing towards King's Lynn, the Wash, and the sea. It is undoubtedly an impressive marriage of forces.

Denver Sluice has been the key to fen drainage for over 300 years and a number of constructions have been necessary to control the South Level at this section. Cornelius Vermuyden recognized the importance of Denver, and drainage engineers throughout the succeeding generations have shared this view. The original sluice ' blew ' in the eighteenth century and most of the surrounding fields were once more drowned under a sea of floodwater. After the disastrous floods of 1947 it was agreed that the plans and ideas that had been talked about for years must be brought into operation whatever the cost—and the cost was going to be staggering. But those early post-war years, for all their grimness, seemed to give people an extra shot of enthusiasm and determination to rebuild cities, cathedrals, schools, new towns, roads, bridges, concert-halls and sluices.

Eventually a new Relief Channel was cut from Denver to King's Lynn and this meant also the building of twenty or so new road bridges, three railway bridges, improving the pumping-station at Wiggenhall St Germans, and enlarging the

Denver Sluice itself by installing powerful new gates. The scheme was completed in 1964 at a cost of nearly £11 million.

Have the waters at last been tamed? It would appear so, and certainly everyone concerned hopes so. As I stand looking over the broad stretch of water on a calm summer's day like this the river looks decidedly docile with its armada of small boats moored along the banks and a few eager fishermen getting the feel again of the rod and line. Later in the season there will be several hundred hopefuls watching the float, hoping to pull out some of the many excellent bream to be fished here, as well as an occasionally weighty chub or perch.

From Denver I travel to Downham Market, an interesting enough little town to pause at for a while but one that has, like many more, become a victim of modern traffic. It has one or two claims to fame in that it helped to educate the young Norfolk boy who was to become Lord Nelson and it was also the home of Captain Manby who invented the life-saving gun used in shore-to-shipwreck rescue operations.

Despite its irritating one-way system and the throb of heavy lorries on their way to and from King's Lynn, Downham Market is still a good gateway into Norfolk. From its crossroads you can turn northwards into the beautiful countryside that leads to royal Sandringham and the coast, or you can turn southwards towards the thickly wooded Thetford Chase and Grimes Graves, or you can continue eastwards to Swaffham and East Dereham, as I am doing today.

It's not the prettiest road in the county by any means, but today I am on a mini-pilgrimage and so decide to keep to the main road for expediency. There are by-roads to Swaffham through Beechamwell Warren and, after the almost treeless fens that we have just left, it is refreshing to see a few acres of trees. In fact Thetford Chase is the largest man-made forest in Europe, containing millions of conifers and some wild deer.

Whether you are on a pilgrimage or not it would be a pity to drift off into north Norfolk without sparing some time for the spacious, airy, relaxed and friendly town of Swaffham which, for a town of its size, surely offers as many free parking spaces as some big cities, or anywhere else for that matter—except on market day, which is an exciting day to be in the town. Certainly I find no difficulty today in parking right outside the shops, where I am treated courteously and helpfully by shop assistants who don't have that look of hatred or contempt for customers that we are accustomed to seeing so often these days, particularly in city shops. There was none of this " If it's not on the shelf we haven't got it ", but " If you'd like to wait a moment I will go and see if I can find one for you upstairs in the stock room ".

Swaffham's history is a long one which goes back to pre-Saxon times. People of the Stone Age, Bronze Age, Iron Age and the Romans have all had settlements within its boundaries, and when our age is only remembered as the Plastic Age, or Pollution Age, the archaeologists of a thousand years' time will no doubt be adding another layer of history to this fascinating town.

In 1836 Swaffham was described as " one of the handsomest and busiest market towns in the county and the principal place of election of Knights of the Shire for the western division of Norfolk. It holds a pleasant and salubrious situation on the ground of lofty eminence ".

I don't suppose travel-writers dare use a word like " salubrious " these days but I have to admit to feeling pretty good and healthy as I explore the place. There is an extra spring in my steps and the smell of newly-baked bread spicing the Norfolk air gives me an appetite.

I have deliberately not said too much about churches in this book so that when I did come across one that I particularly like it would gain something by not having a gazetteer of indifferent competitors. The church of SS. Peter and Paul at Swaffham is one that I am happy to mention because it has several distinctive and praiseworthy features. Beautifully set in a cluster of trees, it invites you into a green coolness and an ancient silence. The double hammer-beam roof is a particularly fine example and made of chestnut. There are, says the guide book, " eighty-eight angels carved on the ends of the hammer-beams and on either side of the king posts all along the top, and a further one hundred and four all along the wall plate on either side. Each of them bearing shields, many of them with the Instruments of the Passion ". The pew-ends too are decorated with an assortment of birds, animals and Apocalyptic figures.

One character inevitably associated with the church, as well as the town itself, is John Chapman, the Swaffham Pedlar and liberal benefactor. There are several versions of the story about the Pedlar but most of them draw on the account recorded in the Abraham de la Pryne Diary:

> Constant tradition says that there lived in former times, in Soffham [Swaffham] *alias* Sopham in Norfolk, a certain pedlar who dreamed that if he went to London Bridge, and stood there, he should hear very joyful news, which he at first sleighted, but afterwards, his dream being doubled and trebled upon him, he resolved to try the issue of it and accordingly went to London and stood on the bridge there two or three days, looking about him, but heard nothing that might yield him any comfort. At last it happened that a shop-keeper there, hard by, having noted his fruitless standing, seeing that he neither sold any wares nor asked any alms, went to him and most earnestly begged to know what he wanted there, or what his business was; to which the pedlar honestly answered that he had dreamed that if he came to London and stood there upon the bridge he should hear good news; at which the shop-keeper laughed heartily, asking him if he was such a fool as to take on such a journey on such a silly errand, adding, " I'll tell thee country fellow, last night I dreamed that I was in Sopham, Norfolk, a place utterly unknown to me, where me thought behind a pedlar's house in a certain orchard, and under a great tree, if I digged, I should find a vast treasure! Now, think you? says he, that I am such a fool to take such a long journey upon me, upon the instigation of a silly dream? No, no, I'm wiser. Therefore, good fellow, learn witt from me and get you home and mind your own business."

So, as you've guessed, the pedlar, being a good and canny countryman, kept his thoughts to himself and hurried back home to Norfolk, and to Swaffham in particular, where he began digging furiously until he " found a prodigious great treasure and grew exceedingly rich ". Swaffham church was then in great need of repair and so the local pedlar donated large sums of money, not only towards its restoration but also towards the building of the north aisle.

> . . . and to this day there is his own statue therein, but in stone, with his pack at his back and his dog at his heels; and his memory is also preserved by the same form or picture in most of the old glass windows, taverns and alehouses of that town until, this day.

A more conspicuous remembrance of the pedlar greets you on a corner of the market place where there is a modern signpost of

Swaffham which shows the pedlar and his dog on their journey. Underneath is the inscription: " Ye Pedlar of Swaffham who did by a dream find a great treasure."

Legend also has it that on finding the first chest of gold John Chapman also discovered some Latin words on the lid which, when translated for him by some students, read

> *Under me doth lie*
> *Another, much richer than I.*

And, when he dug again, to be sure, he found another treasure richer than the first.

Perhaps the moral of this tale is that our riches are always nearer home than we think, that the real wealth is under our nose, not in strange cities or far-off lands. Whatever one makes of the Pedlar legend, John Chapman clearly became a wealthy and generous man who proved that dreams should not be ignored.

The carved village sign is, incidentally, a striking feature of many Norfolk villages. They are carved in wood and decorated with some scene of local significance. The fashion was started on the royal estate at Sandringham in 1912 when George V ordered three new signs to be erected on some of his villages. These were designed by a Mr A. Kingston Rudd and made in the carving school at Sandringham. Most of the other signs in the county have, appropriately enough, been carved by a Mr H. Carter of Swaffham. It is an attractive craft which adds greatly to Norfolk's character and welcome.

The mini-pilgrimage I spoke of a few moments ago, however, was not to the tomb of a Swaffham pedlar but to East Dereham and the tomb of the poet William Cowper, on whom I devoted most of my Huntingdon chapter. But Cowper is such an interesting person that I believe it's worth following his story to the end, linking up all the associations with him in the area.

East Dereham has, in fact, two literary connections— William Cowper and George Borrow, two very different personalities to be sharing some posterity in one small place in Norfolk. Cowper died here; Borrow was born here, in a house on the edge of town.

I shall return to George Borrow a little later when I extend this pilgrimage to his birthplace at Dumpling Green, but my first wish, now that I have arrived in Dereham, is to finish my account of that strange, gentle poet and hymn-writer who occupied my thoughts so much a few chapters ago.

After the happy years at Huntingdon, and the extraordinarily complex life at Olney, William Cowper finally moved to East Dereham in 1796 with the dying Mary Unwin, the woman who had helped him, inspired him, tormented him and worn him, and herself, out. Their last eighteen months together were not happy ones and Cowper sensed that with the loss of Mary his own life was virtually over too. He never recovered from her death, even though he never mentioned her name again. Did he grieve for the unfulfilled love, or the wasted years, for the rare beauty of their relationship, or the sorrow it brought? What price has to be paid for immortal lines or what loneliness endured for a gift of words?

The house where Cowper lived and died was on the market place; it is there no more but in its place stands a Congregational Church known as the William Cowper Memorial church where, no doubt, from time to time some of the poet's hymns are still sung.

> Here may we prove the power of prayer
> To strengthen faith and sweeten care;
> To teach our faint desires to rise
> And bring all Heaven before our eyes.

Cowper died in 1800 and was buried in the parish church, in St Edmund's Chapel. There is a memorial above the tomb and also a stained-glass window, designed by John Flaxman and installed in 1897. It shows the poet reading a book, surrounded by the scenes and creatures that he loved, including his dog and his favourite hare. If the poor, tortured man did not know much tranquillity during his few years at Dereham his memorial at least offers his memory an atmosphere of peace. The chapel evokes a spirit of great gentleness, calm, and care. Today the sunlight makes the window golden. The vase of blue flowers adds to the silence—or, as Cowper would have said, the stillness.

> Stillness, accompanied with sounds so soft,
> Charms more than silence. Meditations here
> May think down hours to moments. Here the heart
> May give an useful lesson to the head,
> And learning wiser grow without his books.

In the same chapel is a memorial to Mary Unwin and the white stones hold for ever now the lifetimes of the two people who were drawn to each other even beyond their understanding. The stillness charms more than the silence. The end of the journey has been reached. The pilgrimage accomplished.

There is much more in this lovely church to admire but the reason for my visit is over. I want the sunlight now and the fresh air. I want the birds singing and the smell of grass. Beyond the stillness and stained glass, beyond the stones and silent words there is a living world of nature that beckons me on to other shrines.

As I walk away I think back over the years and remind myself that William Cowper was one of the first poets I remember reading, certainly one of the first " old poets " as I used to call them when the only other two or three poets I read were still alive. Cowper and John Clare were early discoveries after Dylan Thomas and T. S. Eliot. Clare is a greater poet than Cowper and has undoubtedly had a deeper influence upon me, but I cannot visit Huntingdon, Olney, or Dereham without having a soft spot for the " stricken deer ".

Outside the church, the air is warm and the swallows play hide-and-seek among the tombstones. Not far away a road-drill disturbs the stillness—for not even East Dereham is without its roadworks. It's a twentieth-century disease. Heaps of tar-macadam are piled over the countryside these days like black fungi spreading contagiously into every village and byway, slowly taking us over, adding to our irritations.

Next to the church is an ancient cottage and museum, built in 1502 and now dedicated to Bishop Bonner who was once the vicar of Dereham. It is a fascinating little place, almost fairyland-like in today's setting and changes. My first reaction is one of amazement that a place so old, so rare and so vulnerable should have survived at all.

It is time, however, for me to leave the town of Dereham itself and set off on the other part of my pilgrimage to Norfolk—the birthplace of that considerable word-spinner, George Borrow. In many ways Borrow remains as much an enigma as Cowper, though totally different in personality and style. I have enjoyed rediscovering him and find his travel-writing much more lively than a good deal of what has been written since. At least you know that Borrow's books are written by a human being and not a computer. He reminds us, as Edward Thomas said in his excellent biography published in 1912, that " an author is not bound to be a nun with a beard ".

The author of *The Bible in Spain, Lavengro, The Romany Rye,* and *Wild Wales* was born on 5 July 1803 at a little place on the edge of the town, known then as Dumpling Green. There is, incidentally, an interesting story—again told by Edward Thomas in his volume *Four and Twenty Blackbirds*—of a small boy named " Bob Dumpling of Dumpling Green in Norfolk " who always believed he was the first person to use the couplet " Birds of a feather/Flock together ". It came to him one day when he was being taken by a Thetford drover down to Somerset to see his father. The drover praised Bob as a poet among the other drovers and travellers they met on their way and the phrase was repeated over and over again. Bob did not reach his destination as quickly as some of the travellers he'd met and he was annoyed when he eventually reached Glaston-bury to hear someone else repeating his words. But although he was to hear the phrase many times after that, he still believed he had composed it and that others had stolen it from him. As far as we know it was his only opus and when he died the poet of Dumpling Green was buried in an unknown grave.

Dumpling Green is still only a rough, pot-holed track they call ' the lane ', but all around is a world that would now be quite strange to the more famous author who lived there, the tall, broad-shouldered and muscular figure of George Borrow who, even as a middle-aged man, liked a good, brisk, fifteen-mile walk. He would even go for a long walk in the pouring rain " in case I should lose my appetite for dinner ". I shall return to the subject of his appetite in a moment.

George Borrow was the son of a Captain Thomas Borrow, a Cornishman and professional soldier who had risen from the ranks to be esteemed by his superiors. He married Ann Perfrement, an attractive actress of French descent, and from her George Borrow was to inherit his " continental flair ", his passion and fluctuating temperament.

Because the regiment moved around quite a bit the Borrows' children acquired the habit of travelling at a very early age and George saw much of England, Scotland and Ireland during his school years. In 1816, however, the family returned to Norfolk and settled in Norwich where Borrow became articled to a solicitor. After such a roaming life, and with his natural restlessness, he must have found the lawyer's office very stifling and arid with legal dust. Conveyances, wills and testaments, pink string and sealing wax, belonged to an airless and alien world for a man who loved the open air and trusted the word of gypsies. It is no surprise then that he neglected his law studies and gave more time to his chief passion—languages. By the time he was eighteen he could speak at least twelve languages, including Danish, Spanish, Welsh, Italian, French, Greek and Hebrew. Edward Thomas says in his biography of George Borrow that by the end of his life this largely self-taught man could speak thirty languages and found the mysteries of a strange tongue irresistible. Certainly Borrow was still only a young man when he published translations of Danish ballads, French, Welsh and German poets, and began work on Spanish and Portuguese. In 1833, when still only thirty, he was appointed as an official translator to the British and Foreign Bible Society and, ironically, his first assignment was to translate into a language he did *not* know. He was asked to translate the New Testament into Manchu, the court language of China. With very few books to consult, and no tutor, he learnt the language in three weeks—a man who surely had "the gift of tongues". Sixteen weeks later he passed an examination in Manchu and set off for Russia to work in the St Petersburg libraries—Russia at that time being the only European country represented at the Chinese Court. As if the New Testament were not challenge enough, Borrow also took the opportunity to translate some poetry of Russian, Polish, Persian and Turkish poets. It was as if this giant of a man had to do everything in giant proportions—his work, his walks, and his eating. We read in *Wild Wales* for instance that he sat down to his favourite breakfast of mutton chops, broiled and pickled salmon, eggs, fried trout and potted shrimps. He doesn't mention the toast and marmalade but I bet he would have found room for it. He frequently talks about having " a noble goose for dinner " and usually after a salmon or trout. He also liked drinking ale with his meat. There was certainly no ' starving in a garret ' image for this writer.

After Russia George Borrow turned his attention to Spain and, out of the four and a half years he spent there, he was to write the two books which were to give him some popularity during his lifetime—*Gypsies in Spain* and *The Bible in Spain*. During this time he had also become very friendly with a Mrs Clarke, the woman who had introduced him to the Bible Society, herself now the widow of a naval officer. She was seven years older than Borrow and had a daughter Henrietta, but Borrow knew she was the person with whom he wanted to share his life and they were married on 23 April 1840.

George Borrow never quite fitted into the literary scene of his time and remained something of a mystery among his contemporaries, including the distinguished names of Wordsworth, Tennyson, Browning, Thackeray, Carlyle, the Brontës and Charles Dickens. He did not care for literary parties, for pretence or affectation, for noisy, smoky, over-heated rooms; and he could be very curt in his replies to correspondents, particularly the ladies. The *Romany Rye* lay untouched in his publisher's office for three years before finally going to the printers. A similar reluctance to publish *Wild Wales* meant that the work did not appear until 1862, even though Borrow did the actual journey and research for the book in 1854, returning to Wales on subsequent visits before a word went to the printers. Even when the book did reach the public it received only a very lukewarm reception, and yet he was, as Edward Thomas was to say of him, " a master of the living word ".

The Borrow family moved back to Norfolk, where they had been able to buy some property at Oulton Broad, and there he was able to settle down to his writing and to renew his old acquaintances with the gypsies whose company he so much enjoyed.

His wife died in 1865, and he died on 26 July 1881, not a famous man, but a disappointed one who felt that his work had not been fully appreciated. He was not the first and will certainly not be the last writer to die with that regret in his heart and, as so often happens, his work still lives on while those who criticized him are forgotten. But perhaps, in the end, fame isn't all that important, unless it brings contentment— and the two are rare. Borrow would I think be happy enough to know that *Wild Wales* still sells a few hundred copies each year, that people still set off for Wales with it in their pockets, to retrace his steps, and that more than a hundred years after its publication it is spoken of now as " the best book ever written about Wales ". That can't be a bad achievement or an inadequate share of immortality. To leave behind one classic is as much as any man can hope for and with that one work George Borrow set a new standard in travel-writing that is seldom equalled for freshness, interest and enthusiasm.

*　　*　　*

The green, soothing and tranquil ways of this lovely county of Norfolk, north of Dereham, tempt me on to a longer journey than I expected. But how can you resist the appeals of a countryside that is so complete, so balanced and so inviting? Farms, fields, woods and villages; undulating roads and a network of unspoilt lanes ripening with blackberries; a spirit in the air that slows down time and stretches the hours so that the days *are* longer. The warmth and light. The space and skies. The welcome and the contentment. All are still there in abundance, especially off the main routes, away from the towns, and out of peak season.

I have spent many happy days in Norfolk from when I was a child on summer holidays to more recent times when my work has fortunately granted me time to know it in all its seasons. I have stayed in small cottages, hotels and windmills. I have seen it emerald green in spring and copper-coated in autumn. I have endured gales in winter and have walked over the salt-marshes when it was easy to believe that you were alone on the earth.

It is still one of the most beautiful counties in England and has probably been able to hang on to its real character longer than most because of its geographical position. When I talk to people who have known the county more years than I can remember they tell me that I have already missed the best, that times have changed very much since the war and the atmosphere of the place is not anything like as quiet as it used to be. " Too many people just coming and going now," says one. " You never get to know anybody these days," says another, " they're allus rushing through the place."

Norfolk prides itself on having ' regular visitors ' and by that it means families who have been coming for twenty or thirty years, one generation after another. I know of one family who have spent every summer holiday since the war in Cromer and had all their childhood holidays there before the war came to hasten the changes. The same can be said of other families who have gone back year after year to Great Yarmouth, or Sheringham, or Hunstanton. The reasons why they go vary slightly, but usually amount to something that they can only describe as "certainty" or "familiarity"; "a feeling of relaxation and well-being"; of "welcome" or "it's like home from home without the worries". Some go for the brisk sea air, for the unhurried life-style, for the peace, the long days, the good food. One old farmer I know always goes "for the sake of my bowels . . . it's better than any salts. A fortnight in Hunstanton or Sheringham sets me up for the year". What more can you ask of a holiday?

A recent survey has shown that people in north Norfolk do in fact live longer on average than people in any other part of Britain and maybe in Europe. For the size of its population there are more over-eighties in this part of the country than anywhere else and to have your hundredth birthday here does not have quite the same distinction as it does in other areas. Some say it's no more than "good, wholesome food and no tearing about"; and some say it's "because of what's in the soil—and that's our secret!" There are others who say "it's all to do with natural selectivity, nothing else; only the fittest have ever survived in Norfolk since time began and so we all come from good stock, you see! If you notice, it's only the locals 'at live so long!"

Well, I can take a hint and hereby warn all those who might wish to prolong their lives *not* to rush up for a house in Norfolk now—you've left it too late.

* * *

Not very far from East Dereham on the road to Fakenham is the village of North Elmham, which is one of those compelling, don't-pass-it-by villages that draws you into its web of history. There is an atmosphere that says "Wait a moment, for we have things to tell you! Wait, and let our stones speak to you!"

And some of the first stones you look for in North Elmham belong to the ruins of a Saxon cathedral, an East Anglian See from 673 to 1075. Even allowing for later additions, for repairs and its now shadowy history, there is undoubtedly something very captivating about these excavations. The rough, coarse, heavy, solid stones that make up these walls and towers were clearly meant to withstand any threat. They may not, in the end, have withstood the determined hands of destruction and change, but what remains is still very exciting. There is a sense of antiquity here, an atmosphere that is, I feel, more pagan than Christian. You can't help thinking of Druids rather than monks. There are echoes of rituals, shivers of mystery and powerful silences. But they are different from those felt in the ruins of abbeys like Croyland, Fountains or Bolton. I find myself enthralled by the site, by the solid walls of what is left. It *feels* old. It's marvellous to touch. There are darknesses into which you cannot see even though you are stepping back into the shadows of thirteen hundred years ago.

After 1075 the See of East Anglia was transferred to Thetford and, eventually, in 1096, to Norwich. Just over ten years ago the title of Bishop of Elmham was revived by the Roman Catholic Church for its assistant bishop in the Diocese of Northampton.

Later excavations have revealed that a large Saxon settlement once existed at North Elmham and there is a definite feeling here today that I am walking in buried footsteps, shaking hands over the centuries with those who breathed Norfolk's air over a thousand years ago.

The parish church too is of exceptional interest and must go on my short-list of ' ones-not-to-be-missed '—though in a county like Norfolk so rich in church building it is difficult to have a short-list. This one will not disappoint ' when you enter in ', and when you descend the steps into the nave you are again entering a world that stimulates the imagination.

Norfolk always looks so clean, and today the flint cottages and churches sparkle in the bright sunlight. Every road is an adventure. The narrow, hedge-high lanes, the green avenues of trees, the wide rolling fields, the farms, crops, cattle and wild flowers, all combine to make this a perfect landscape. Again, away from the obvious places, and except at weekends, it is still a joy to motor quietly on its unfrequented roads. I clocked fourteen miles this morning without seeing another car and passed no more than seven or eight vehicles in three hours. Drivers more familiar with the busy trunk roads in the west of the region may find this hard to believe, but it's true. There are, I believe, more cars on the road in Norfolk than in any other county, but fortunately for me they are mostly going to Norwich or down to Ipswich, Newmarket or Harwich.

*   *   *

Having discovered the Tollbridge Restaurant at Guist earlier in the morning, we return to it for lunch after our explorations into those uncharted ways. We receive an excellent meal from a kitchen that cares. There is a good menu, some good wines, friendly service and a setting by the River Wensum that lets you dine in tranquillity. Hot Norfolk cockles in lemon and butter sauce have never tasted better and the beef cooked in red wine has a rich, succulent taste to savour.

And so the day continues, towards Fakenham (an interesting little market town with one or two unusual shops and a good place for browsers); on to Walsingham (famous today again for its pilgrimages, though any sense of awe always eludes me); and finally on to Wells-next-the-Sea (which at times seems to be a long way from the sea when the tide is out). Even so, Wells has the true air of a harbour town and offers a good mixture of the raw and the sophisticated. It still has character—Norfolk character—and there is a certain excitement in the blood as I approach this part of the Norfolk coast.

I can see the sea in the distance, between the roof-tops of the town. I slow down. I feel tired. The mind has received as much as it can in one day. It is time to pause. Time to reflect. Time to breathe in the sea air and let the rest of the journey wait, for, in the words of Edward Thomas again—who seems to have been my literary companion on this pilgrimage—

> I have come to the borders of sleep,
> The unfathomable deep
> Forest where all must lose
> Their way, however straight,
> Or winding, soon or late;
> They cannot choose . . .

*   *   *

10

A Touch of Class

Along the coast from Wells to Hunstanton are a string of individual little places worth discovering. They are like coloured beads on an abacus and you can count them off slowly, one by one: Holkham, with its famous house, gardens and pottery; Overy Staithe; Burnham Norton; Burnham Deepdale; Brancaster; Thornham; Holme-next-the-Sea; and Old Hunstanton.

Holkham Hall attracts thousands of holiday-makers who want to see one of the great houses of Norfolk. It was built by William Kent between 1734 and 1761 for the Earl of Leicester, whose nephew ' Coke of Norfolk ' transformed acres of barren land into good farming land, and did much to revolutionize English agriculture. Nikolaus Pevsner said of Holkham Hall: " it is more consistently palatial than that of almost any other house in England ". The parklands were laid out by that artist of landscape-gardening, Capability Brown, who was also responsible for many of the great parks in the area and is buried in the quiet little village of Fenstanton, near Cambridge.

I cannot pass Overy Staithe without giving it some part of my day because I have in the past enjoyed many solitary hours among its creeks and on its marshes. There is a calm wildness here where the earth and sky seem to belong only to the warm wind and the sea-birds' cries. Human beings are there too, in their cars, their boats and plimsolls, but they are dwarfed by the wildness of nature.

This section of the Norfolk coast has a special place in my affections too because of the black tower windmill on the Burnham Overy road. I have spent many contented hours under those white sails and after a day out on the marshes it was a great comfort to return to the safety and cosiness of its thick, warm walls, to the gentle glow of oil-lamps and candles, and the smell of supper and a newly-lit fire. In *The Solitary*

The William Cowper memorial window in East Dereham church

IN MEMORY
OF MARY WIDOW OF
THE REVEREND MORLEY UNWIN
AND MOTHER OF
THE REVEREND WILLIAM CAWTHORNE UNWIN
BORN AT ELY 1724
BURIED IN THIS CHURCH 1796.

TRUSTING IN GOD WITH ALL HER HEART & MIND
THIS WOMAN PROV'D MAGNANIMOUSLY KIND
ENDUR'D AFFLICTION'S DESOLATING HAIL
AND WATCH'D A POET THRO' MISFORTUNES VALE
HER SPOTLESS DUST ANGELIC GUARDS DEFEND
IT IS THE DUST OF UNWIN, COWPER'S FRIEND
THAT SINGLE TITLE IN ITSELF IS FAME
FOR ALL WHO READ HIS VERSE REVERE HER NAME

Memorial tablet to Mary Unwin, in East Dereham church

George Borrow's birthplace, Dumpling Green

The Customs House, King's Lynn

North Brink, Wisbech

The 'Chinese Bridge', Godmanchester

The River Great Ouse, near Godmanchester

The Mill, Houghton

Hemingford Grey

Landing-stage on the Great Ouse

Autumn clouds begin to gather . . .

The end of a season; a deserted farm cottage

Landscape I recalled one autumn night when a strong wind was blowing in over a full tide and how we sat happily huddled in the silence and strength of the old mill:

> Above us the sails are fixed in silence.
> Mist anchors our ark to the sea-bed of barley
> As we gather round a table of bright words . . .
> Then, fading the bloom of oil-lamps into night,
> We let our bodies drift into the depths of sleep.

The memory of that night returns with the smell of samphire and wood-smoke, with echoes of other summers when the sun never seemed to desert us or lose its warmth.

The Domesday Book lists seven Burnhams within a radius of two miles, all " by-the-sea " and all with churches. Three of those churches have disappeared and the receding sea has left the villages rather stranded. The most famous of the Burnhams today is Burnham Thorpe where Horatio Nelson was born in 1758.

Brancaster is a favourite place of many visitors to Norfolk, particularly painters and yachtsmen. I prefer the quieter and more solitary marshes at Thornham where there is that indefinable magic in the air and the light somehow more golden, especially in the evening when the sun is setting low beyond the reeds and grasses. Then a new ' sea ' washes in over these untamed acres, a 22-carat sea of light that dazzles the eyes.

Inland from this coastal road there are several lovely drives or walks. Your time is what you make it and, with the Norfolk skylarks overhead, the smell of Norfolk lavender in the air and the sweet grass around you, you can make it a time to enrich your life for ever.

At Holme-next-the-Sea you meet up again with the ancient Peddars Way which stretches as straight as a plumb-line over the width of the county without passing through any other town or village than Castle Acre. If anyone wanted to plan a motorway from just west of Thetford to Holme they couldn't choose a straighter line than the 2,000-year-old route—but heaven forbid such a thought becoming a reality! Norfolk, once safely cut off from all the great commercial highways, is rapidly being ' opened up ' to accommodate the extra heavy vehicles taking cargoes to the continent. Fortunately, at the moment, the Peddars Way only leads you to a few caravan sites and the Wash. If, and when, the Wash Barrier materializes, then this corner of Norfolk will certainly lose its character.

But today is not a day for gloomy speculation or despair. It is enough to rejoice, to praise and to say to any despoilers: "Please leave it alone and let this precious piece of England be preserved for others to enjoy in all its naturalness."

As I reach the broad stretch of sand at Old Hunstanton, with its cliffs and lighthouse, I am reminded of the times I have walked along this shore for miles, without any sign of the twentieth century near me, like, for instance, that day when I walked from Hunstanton to Brancaster, discovering Thornham on the way. It was a day that Edward Thomas or George Borrow would have enjoyed, with good ale and cheese to satisfy the appetite.

Hunstanton, or 'Hunstan' as it was always called locally, especially on the railways, used to be to the farm-workers and brickyard workers of Cambridgeshire what Blackpool was, I suppose, to the cotton-workers of Lancashire. During the 'twenties and 'thirties Hunstan was the place to which people flocked for their one week's holiday. Sometimes, of course, the money would not run to a full week at a boarding-house and holidays were restricted to 'days-only', to the works' outing or Sunday school outing.

But somehow, by train or bus, hundreds of families did escape from the brick-dust and harvest fields to make their annual pilgrimage to the sea to "set themselves up for the rest of the year".

I remember some of my first visits when I was a small child and a trip to Hunstanton meant not only a day at the sea but also a journey in a train. The station was a good mile from where we lived but I can remember now the thrill of each step as we crossed the market square and hurried down to the little platform with its flower-beds, gas-lamps and row of red fire-buckets outside the 'gents'. There I would wait impatiently, staring at the two shining lines that curved away into the unifying distance, studying the sky for a blur of smoke that would announce the approaching train. The porter would look at his watch, glance at the signals and forecast to a second the moment when the train would appear from behind a cluster of trees and arrive, puffing and panting, into our station. His knowledge and power impressed me tremendously when I was five or six. What impressed me even more was the train, breathing fire and steam as it waited for us to climb aboard with our buckets and spades, our cases and carrier-bags, our packets of sandwiches and bottles of lemonade. Then the whistle would blow and the engine would tug us slowly away from the familiar fields and over the fens to the sea. In the corridorless compartment I would examine the water-colours of castles or harbours that were fixed above the long seats and dream of worlds I never thought I would see; or I would watch the rise and fall of the telegraph wires that gave one the feeling of bouncing along like a stone over water in the game of 'ducks and drakes' we played by the river. Beyond those up-and-down wires the July sun went on ripening the fields of wheat and barley. The long dykes lowered their water level and left the mud-banks dry while the limp and flimsy poppies embroidered the railway embankments. And the sky stretched its cloudless leagues over those eternally blue, hot, summer days all the way into Norfolk and the waiting waves.

Hunstanton still retained then something of its quiet Victorian gentility and I loved every street, shop, pebble and sandcastle it possessed. The memory of sitting on the green one day to eat our sandwiches is as vivid as if it had happened yesterday, and yet I know that I could not have been more than five years old. It was on this spot that St Edmund, King of East Anglia, set foot just before becoming King—not that I knew anything about that particular event then. But you can understand, perhaps, why the place has had the affection of many families for three and four generations; it has been a tradition for years, and still is, even though there is no railway now and everyone arrives by road in their cars or comes in coaches that can never have the same magic of those steam-pulled carriages with their romantic water-colours and stiff leather straps on the windows.

There were also two special observations which had to be made each year: one was to see Boston Stump on the other side of the Wash, twenty miles away, and the other was to see the sun setting over the sea at what is, after all, an east coastal resort. The fact is, that Hunstanton is really a *west*-coastal resort in East Anglia, and so it is possible to watch the sun going down over the water. And, as with much of East Anglia, you still get spectacular sunsets on this part of Norfolk's coastline.

I have a recurring dream of some small holiday village I must have been taken to when I was very young, before the memories themselves began to bury each moment in the mind's silt. I'm certain that it was somewhere near the sea and always I am waiting outside the same shop—an old-fashioned shop with a wooden veranda painted white. It's something of a cross between a small Victorian railway station and a wild-west saloon. The shopkeeper always comes to look at me. He has a waxed moustache, a white apron, and very dark eyes. It's always summer, and I usually end up with a brightly painted bucket or a mechanical duck. I've tried so hard to remember where that shop could have been and I am convinced that it must have been somewhere on the Norfolk coast.

Was it Hunstanton, I wonder? Or Heacham? Or Snettisham? —all places where I spent a few weeks of my infancy! It's not in Hunstanton now, and when I go down to Heacham the concentration of caravans convinces me that if the shop was there once it is certainly not there any more; nor do I find anything like it at Snettisham. I suppose that I am expecting too much after all these years, and I'm sure it is better for the dream to be unresolved.

So now I make my way towards King's Lynn, through Dersingham and then Sandringham. It need hardly be said that at Sandringham we are in one of the most well-known and most visited places in Norfolk. Because of its connections with the Royal Family thousands of visitors come every year to see something of the 20,000-acre estate, with its house, gardens, and church. Few go away unrewarded. It is very beautiful, particularly when the rhododendrons are in full bloom, and the woodland rides are sweet with new vegetation and pine-needles.

The tiny church is inevitably full of royal associations and there is an intimacy about the place that is never lost. Out of season it is possible to sit there alone and share in the pew's memories. Both George V and George VI died at Sandringham and the church has been the focus of a nation's mourning as well as a place of celebration. It is at Sandringham that the monarchy and people come close together without all the usual glitter, pomp, ceremony, fanfares and formality of the city.

Sandringham, Dersingham, Castle Rising—the names ring like a peal of bells on a summer Sunday morning. It is so easy to miss Castle Rising and the lovely Ling Common if you can't resist the dash of speed offered by King's Lynn's bypass, but it is worth delaying the departure from rural Norfolk for another hour or so to explore this very interesting village—a village that was once far more important than its busy neighbour of today:

> Rising was a seaport town
> When Lynn was but a marsh.
> Now Lynn it is a seaport town
> And Rising fares the worse.

So runs an old rhyme which records the changing fortunes of the two places. Rising's prosperity came in the days when the River Babingley was tidal and ships could navigate their way up to its quaysides. There was a time when the village was important enough to enjoy the status of a borough, have a mayor, and two Members of Parliament—Samuel Pepys, then Sir Robert Walpole.

The ruins of the castle also speak of Rising's history and significance. The mighty fortification was built during the reign of King Stephen, in the middle of the twelfth century, and there is still a magnificent stone stairway that rises steeply through a sequence of perfectly proportioned arches. From the high windows of the ruins you look now over the peaceful village, over a pattern of lovely red roofs and the distant Wootten marshes fading into the horizon of sea.

Also in the village is The Hospital of the Most Holy and Undivided Trinity—not a hospital in the modern sense of the word but a place of refuge for " aged and single ladies who could no longer find a home in the remaining convents ". They had to be " of honest life and conversation, religious, grave and discreet . . ." The hospital was built by Henry Howard, Earl of Northampton, and it is an excellent example of early seventeenth-century planning and brickwork. Although there has been some interior modernization the entrance gate, courtyard, dining-hall and chapel remain very much as they have always been. There is also a room with the original Jacobean panelling and a Treasury chest in which the town's wealth was stored and protected from the vagrants, robbers and rogues attracted to a seaport.

The rest now is a memory. Castle Rising became a victim, first of a receding sea, then a receding trade. The River

Babingley became a stream and King's Lynn gained the monopoly of the sea trade.

Looking at Lynn today you cannot imagine it otherwise. It has become a lively and attractive place with its docks, festivals, markets and shops. It isn't all 'olde worlde' and pretty, of course. There are the industrial buildings, the fertilizer manufacturers, canning factories, sugar-beet refineries and an enormous volume of traffic using the docks. But the town 'pulsates', as they say, and the ancient parts of Lynn cannot fail to lead you back into another world of wealthy wool-merchants and the Hanseatic League, to a world of sailing ships and salty sea-captains. Walking some of those narrow cobbled lanes and footpaths you hear echoes of the Middle Ages as clear as your own footsteps. Looking down St Margaret's Lane is like looking through a keyhole into the fifteenth century. You break the time-barrier.

I always find Lynn a stimulating place to visit because it is so alive with both the past and the present, especially on market days. The many stalls, with their many wares and characters, continue an ancient tradition and bring a cosmopolitan atmosphere to the town. The Tuesday Market Place is one of the largest and finest market squares in England and you can have a day's free entertainment just walking about watching and listening to the transactions. The crowded avenues, the babble of noise, the mixture of smells and the vibrating colours; the vegetables, pots, pans, china, dresses, plants and knick-knacks; the meat-stalls, fish-stalls, sausages and cheeses; the lengths of brightly coloured material waving like banners at a Tudor tournament; the tomatoes, grapes, carrots and bananas; the apples, oranges, grapefruit and lettuces; the snowdrifts of gypsophila and explosion of roses; all contributing to a scene of down-to-earth splendour.

King John granted a charter to Lynn in 1204, making the town "a free burgh" with special powers to control its water-borne goods. Henry III was responsible for having the estuary deepened and widened so that more trade could be received, and soon Lynn's port was to be ranked as the third largest in England. When Edward III sent an expedition to France in 1347, Lynn's share of the fleet was nineteen ships, second to London's twenty-four. Two years later Edward visited his "loyal port of Lynn" and was entertained at a banquet given by Robert Braunch, at which peacock was one of the meats served.

There are many dates, places and people to think about on a visit to Kings's Lynn—the Trinity Guildhall, the Customs House, Hampton Court, Clifton House, St Margaret's Church, St Nicholas' Chapel, the Hanseatic Warehouse, the Greenland Fisheries Museum, and a dozen doorways, windows and arches on which you will find carved some reminder of the town's history—all keep the imagination busy as you walk through Lynn's past. So, too, do several of the people who have been its residents by birth or adoption.

Margery Kempe was born in Lynn in 1373 and became a remarkable woman-mystic of her time. Although she could not read or write she dictated her autobiography to a priest and so became the author of one of the most intimate and honest life stories ever written: *The Book of Margery Kempe*. She also travelled widely and was unafraid to speak her mind. She had visions and heard voices; she renounced a life of comfort and marriage for one of poverty and celibacy; and she was believed to be responsible for a number of miracles in the town.

Another famous daughter of Lynn was Fanny Burney who was born in 1752 and earned distinction as a diarist and novelist. Her novels included *Evelina* and *Cecilia* and she counted among her friends Reynolds, Sheridan, Burke, and Dr Johnson. Her father was the musicologist and organist of St Margaret's, Dr Charles Burney, who was also the father of Captain James Burney, the explorer who sailed with Captain Cook.

Lynn could clearly not be satisfied with one famous sailor and produced another in Captain George Vancouver, who was born in 1757 and also sailed with Cook. In 1790 he was appointed to command an expedition " for acquiring a more complete knowledge than has yet been obtained of the north-west coast of America . . . with respect to the nature and extent of any water communication which may tend to facilitate an intercourse for the purpose of Commerce between the north-west coast and the country upon the opposite side of the continent ". As a result of Captain Vancouver's voyages, charts and records, the whole of the coast of north-west America became navigable and his name was given immortality in Vancouver Island.

Lynn continued its great tradition of breeding courageous

sea-captains and Samuel Gurney Cresswell became the first man to traverse the American continent from west to east and to reach England alive, and all before he was forty.

A native explorer who went in the opposite direction on his journeys to Australia was Thomas Baines, a man who comes up to the image of the stubborn, independent and fearless adventurers of the nineteenth century. Nothing daunted him and he considered himself quite an expert in bush-fighting, jungle medicine, painting, gold-mining, photography and boat-building. He died in Africa in 1875, unsung and unrecognized in this country for any of his talents.

Other natives of Lynn have gone into the history books for different reasons. Norfolk, like most of East Anglia, was rather zealous during the sixteenth and seventeenth centuries for its witch-hunting. Matthew Hopkins and John Stearne are still names that can send a shiver down the spine of most East Anglians for these two men decided it was their task to purge their counties of all witches. They toured the countryside and paid for informers. They held assizes in Lynn, Ely, March, Chatteris, Downham, Bury St Edmunds and Great Yarmouth. More than 200 arrests were made, all were tortured for confessions, and over ninety of those found guilty were hanged. A more detailed and gripping account of this awful period can be found in Enid Porter's absorbing volume *The Folklore of East Anglia*.

Not all the so-called witches ended up at the end of a rope; some were burned at the stake, and King's Lynn witnessed such an event in 1590 when Margaret Read was " burned alive until she was dead " in Tuesday Market Place. Lynn sent another witch to her death in 1626 when it hanged Mary Smith, a woman who seemed to be no more than a wicked nuisance to her neighbours.

But enough of the macabre. Lynn has also had its share of famous visitors whose presence has been more welcomed and more gratefully remembered—from Shakespeare and Defoe to Dickens and Dorothy L. Sayers. In more recent years, because of its now acclaimed festival, the town has attracted many distinguished names from the world of the arts—Benjamin Britten, Vaughan Williams, John Betjeman, Peter Ustinov, Sybil Thorndyke, Sir John Barbirolli and many, many more who have found it a friendly and happy place to know.

The locals take it all in their stride—the markets, festivals, visitors, congestion, inconvenience, excitement and publicity, as if it's quite normal to be the object of so much attention. Most of them have a pride in their small, lively and ' let's-get-on-with-it ' town, even if it is occasionally expressed in understatements.

I asked one man on the Market Place what he thought of Lynn and his answer was " It's all right, why?" I asked another and he said, " You've got to admit, it's got a touch of class, that it has."

"A touch of class . . ." How true! How apt! How well expressed with the right mixture of Norfolk modesty and pride. And, after these last few days, it's a phrase I could apply again to much of the county.

*   *   *

At Lynn the Great Ouse reaches the end of its journey and divides two very different landscapes. I look back down the river towards Denver and remember the lovely warm lanes I have travelled on the one side and the straight open roads of the fen country on the other. These are the roads that call now as we approach the end of a summer; roads that dissect the great farmlands of Cambridgeshire and lead back home. New bridges and new dual carriageways now take the traveller away from King's Lynn quicker than he could have left a few years ago. I am reluctant to leave, to enter into the competition again of having a place on trunk roads, but the time to return has come and there are many moments I want to record while the pictures are clear in my mind.

The season is not quite over but already the fields are being cleared, some reploughed, and there is an early autumn clarity in the air.

> The light stretches a long way today
> pushing the clouds to other continents,
> and fields look twice their size because the sun
> touches horizons twenty miles away.
>
> Black furrows merge towards a stranded house
> shining like some small spider in its web.
> Potato-pickers on a distant farm
> could be wild flowers bending in the wind.

A tractor pulls a parachute of gulls
to check its landing-speed before it turns
to plough new flights of soil, while in the sky
larks make again a rainbow of bright sound.

And in backyards, or on some new estate,
greenhouses flash with rich chrysanthemums
giving the day such things to celebrate
that winter dares not come to spoil earth yet.

*   *   *

Between King's Lynn and Wisbech is an area known as
Marshland, an area that has been mainly reclaimed from the
sea and which has certainly been a victim of the sea. Wisbech
was, after all, itself once a seaport and the sea has on several
occasions tried to win back the land it has lost. There are still a
number of ancient sea-walls to be seen in Marshland and some
of the churches carry their own stories of the sea's invasions.

Marshland is noted for its many fine churches: Walsoken,
West Walton, Walpole St Peter, Terrington St Clement, to
mention only four of the most popular. Almost any by-road that
will get you off the busy A47 for a while is worth taking for it
will lead you to a quiet, forgotten world where time seems not
only to have stood still, but to have died. The epitaphs, half
nibbled away by moss on the gravestones, appear to be not so
much for individuals as for the human race.

If you do not want to be reminded of total extinction, then
keep going to Wisbech, for throughout summer, and at fruit-
picking time, Wisbech is proof that we are all still alive. Once
again it is a town that most people pass through rather than
explore, which is a pity because there are undoubtedly a few
corners worth discovering. The museum, the market place, the
church, the park and the North Brink with its good buildings
and Peckover House in particular.

This row of Georgian houses adds considerable distinction to
the town and Peckover House is undoubtedly one of its major
attractions, belonging now to the National Trust. The house
was built in 1722 for the Southwell family but was later bought
by Jonathan Peckover, a local banker. In fact the house was
known then as Bank House, and the firm of Gurney, Birbeck
and Peckover retained its independence until their bank

merged with Barclays in 1896. In 1877 the property passed to Jonathan Peckover's nephew, Alexander, who became Lord Lieutenant of Cambridgeshire and was eventually raised to the peerage as Lord Peckover of Wisbech. He was an enthusiastic collector and bibliophile so the house acquired many riches. The interior still offers a wealth of good design, decoration, Sheraton furniture and paintings.

The road out of Wisbech now follows the brown and sluggish course of the Nene and the once-busy seaport is left to be a place through which thousands of people pass each week on their way to Norfolk and the sea. The roads are noisy and there is little escape from the traffic as I make my way back to Peterborough through Guyhirne and Thorney.

When I wrote of Thorney a few years ago I said it was an oasis between one kind of fen country and another and typical of neither. It still retains that individuality and is a bridge between the Cambridgeshire and Lincolnshire fens, between the rich farming land of the Isle of Ely and the swarming industrial growth of the city of Peterborough. Some of the lovely old trees have disappeared since I last described Thorney but the rest of the village remains in good shape with well-kept stone houses of a past age on the one hand and a modern housing estate on the other. The abbey, which was founded as a Benedictine monastery in 662, is still there and there is now a wildlife park, founded more recently, which attracts the greater number of visitors. The quieter voice of history, however, is what appeals to me and an evening sitting in the garden of Hugh and Renate Cave, drinking German wine until the sun goes down, gives me that link with the past when Thorney was " the flower of many fair tree " and the monks at the monastery made their own fine white wine which was the envy of Crowland and Medehamstede.

The abbey bell gently reminds me of the time—and time in Thorney goes quicker than anywhere else—though perhaps the company and the talking, the contentment and the cellar have something to do with it. But such hours are reality and the harsh lights of the city are unreality. It is a paradox I think I have posed before and thankfully the stars and sleep do not insist on a solution. If our dreams are real enough, why worry! " Dreams are true while they last," wrote Tennyson. " And do we not all live in dreams?"

11

Trees Singing with Children and an Owl's Cry

I met an acquaintance the other day, someone I'd known thirty-five years or more ago, a man who was, as Hilaire Belloc would have said, " a boy when I was a boy ", and soon we were leaning like old sages over a familiar bridge, staring into the stream we had stared in together many summers past, remembering the town, the schools, the boys, the characters and events of those days in Whittlesey that were part of our childhood.

The sunlight gold-plated the water; the warmth stroked our backs; the smell of meadows, river and nettles took our minds back to days of fishing and kite-flying, to a hazy world of heatwaves and holidays. Rooks argued in nearby trees as they had done then and in the distance we could hear the bell of St Mary's Church tolling for a funeral.

The spinney that runs parallel with the stream is known as the Bower. It is not as dense or quite as long as it was then, nor as wild. Some of its old trees have gone, the undergrowth is sparser and more threadbare, and new houses have crept too near for it ever to be a wilderness again. But all those years ago I'm sure it was different—popular by day with the boys for bird's-nesting, cowboys and Indians, and other adventures, and equally popular at night with those who had outgrown the cops and robbers stage but had not yet reached the comfort of the marriage bed.

The bower was legendary for its evils, rape, murder, suicide and witchcraft. We listened to the grown-ups gossip with our mouths wide open and a rising pulse rate. The next adventure there would be even more daring. To travel through the Bower on a dark night was as exciting as any jungle. Lovers groaned on iron seats and we could eavesdrop on the inarticulate passions and sighings of the anonymous bodies wrestling in the dark. We put names to unknown faces. We coupled the most unlikely characters together and tried to add our own fantasies to the gossip of the town.

When the war came it was even better. If there was a lull in the amorous activities of our elders we could stalk invisible German spies through the trees, freezing with fear as each snapped twig became a threat, the click of a gun or the flick of a knife.

" Do you remember that time when we found a life-size effigy of Hitler hanging from the roof of the pill-box at the Briggate end of the Bower?"

" That's right, and someone had driven a wooden stake through his chest . . . we never went there again."

Our day-time activities took us beyond the Bower into the great open fens where we used to fly our kites. If the wind was right these kites of ours would slowly soar away over the velvet-black fields, pulling further and further away as we added more string. As the hand tugged gently at the pulling kite you could feel the string slowly burning into your hand. Someone had told us that if we threaded a key on to the string it would gradually make its way up to the top. We tried this once and watched with fascination as the key slowly inched its way along the loop of string until it reached a knot and had to stop.

Our kites were not the little plastic things you buy at seasides today but huge creatures made of coloured cloth and cane, with tails several feet long. To see them rising free of the earth to share an hour with the skylarks and clouds was an elation I shall never forget. They lifted our minds from the fields and the brickyard chimneys, from those places where we thought we might have to spend the rest of our lives.

To give up those afternoon pleasures of kite-flying or fishing to sit in a stuffy Victorian classroom was unbearable, but we knew that part of life was important too if we wanted to do well for ourselves. Ambition was a poor consolation for freedom in those days and I felt terribly frustrated at being shut away from the summer fields.

*   *   *

" Shall we go for a drink?" my acquaintance said, and we made our way to a pub near the railway station.

On the way, we tried to remember as many of the pub names there used to be then in the town. The Hero of Aliwal, The Hare and Hounds, The Queen Adelaide, The Three Fishes, The Black Swan, The Packhorse, The White Horse, The Woolpack, The Boat, The Letter A, and The Letter B, and all the others that made up the fifty-two pubs that once bred their own characters, traditions and legends of great drinkers.

We passed what used to be our recreation ground and it's a place I can never pass without remembering a dream I once had about the place just before the war. I was sitting in the long grass watching some older children on the swings. They worked themselves higher and higher until, at each peak of their upward surge, they became momentarily lost in a row of trees. Later in my dream, I saw the swings come down without the children until, one by one, all the children disappeared. As darkness came I watched all the mothers enter the recreation field looking for their children. They were crying and bewildered. They called for their children, but the recreation ground remained silent. Only I could hear the trees singing with children; but I could not tell the mothers for in my dream I was dumb and my mouth was a hollow out of which no sound came.

* * *

The approach to the railway station reminded us of another event that happened one Sunday morning soon after war was declared, a morning when the evacuees started arriving from London and were assembled in our school to wait for ' other parents' to claim them.

Many of the children were crying and, in the bright sunlight of that Sunday morning, I remember how pale their faces looked compared with ours. Clutching their few belongings, including their gas-masks, they were sorted out into groups, ages, families, sizes and sex. They had identity labels tied to their jackets and looked, as they were, the pitiful victims of some terrible indignity.

Slowly, out of the confusion and crying, some order came as the children were handed over to local people who were to provide them with a home. Although the women kept saying

" Bless their hearts ", there was little comfort for the children that morning, and the kind words uttered in a coarse tenderness must have frightened them as much as comforted them. " Now doan't yew be frit of us boy cus yew'll be orlroight once we git yew 'um; just yew git in that ole car and stop yer blabbering. We've got a houseful of litluns loike yew at'll be able to play wi' yer."

The boy was driven away to a small-holding on the edge of town and, after the crowded streets of the East End of London, it must have felt like Siberia. I got to know him later when he came to our school and, after that first year, he enjoyed helping to feed the pigs and chickens at his new home. I've forgotten his name, and the people who cared for him are no longer there.

The evacuees reminded us of the war and our own ' Dad's Army '—the Local Defence Volunteers who became our Home Guard. We used to go down to the Manor Field on Sunday afternoons to watch them training and they would have us in fits of laughter as they charged around with pitchforks, rakes and broom-handles. When someone offered them a vaulting-horse for their training-sessions it is reputed that one of the unsung heroes was heard to say: " I don't care what breed it is, you won't get me to ride it." On another occasion one of our courageous defenders was asked what he would do if, alone, he came face to face with a pack of German invaders? His reply was confident and reassuring. " What I'd do first, Sir, is surround them and make them surrender . . ."

But these were early days and we were soon to be as proud of our Home Guard and Army Cadets as any in the fens. And it really was every town or village for itself, for rival villages vowed they would not defend each other.

*   *   *

The beer tasted cool and refreshing as we sat by an open window of the bar and continued our reminiscing.

" Another thing that used to make me laugh was those practice runs down to the air-raid shelters which were about half a mile from the classroom anyway."

" True. D'you remember that time when I was threatened with all hell's tortures for leaving my gas-mask behind in the classroom, a mistake for which I was personally grateful when I finally got to the shelter and heard the rest of you trying to sing

' Speed bonny boat like a bird on the wing . . .' through your bizarre head-gear. When I couldn't control my laughter I'm sure the teacher was convinced that our rehearsal had turned into reality and I was a victim of one of Hitler's secret chemicals."

" We were lucky, weren't we. The only real excitement came when a convoy of tanks rumbled through town or a stray German bomber was caught in the thin searchlight beams from one of the ack-ack units stationed nearby."

" But we did ' Dig for Victory ', if you remember, on the site of the old work-house."

" Aye! All I can remember growing was a row of radishes. I wonder if they helped us to win the war?"

" And we entertained the troops in the chapel-schoolroom after the evening service on Sunday."

" Some entertainment . . . an old tea-urn, some sticky buns and some even stickier musical items—' Bless This House ', ' The Holy City ', and ' If I Can Help Somebody '."

" But it was good fun at the time and some of the soldiers used to come home with us afterwards for supper, a glorious fry-up of all that was left from Sunday lunch—cabbage, peas, potatoes, bread, the last rasher of bacon and a slice of Spam, all making a pan full of food that spat and sizzled on the old black stove and then came steaming to the table to be eaten by everyone with uninhibited relish. Sometimes there would be enough eggs to go round and, with a large bottle of Daddy's Sauce to add a little spice, you could be sure of going to bed with a full stomach."

I also remembered that by this time we had an old piano which filled one corner of our small front room. It had brass candlesticks and a fret-worked front, keys as cracked and yellow as prehistoric teeth, and a lid that weighed as heavy as a lead coffin. I was having piano lessons from a man who used to provide the music in the local cinema during the silent film era—which in our town then wasn't so very long ago. We haven't got a cinema of any kind now, so why should I scoff? My music-teacher looked a bit like Paderewski and I frequently wondered what change of fortune had made his long white fingers turn to thrashing out suitable ' chase music ' for Westerns or ' sob music ' for tear-jerkers instead of Chopin or Mozart in the Queen's Hall. The fact that he never got me beyond a hurly-burly piece called 'Fire! Fire!' probably explains his limitations. On the other hand, perhaps I was unteachable. When my rendering of this one piece caused my parents many moments of anguish and despair I used to blame the piano, but when one of the soldiers we invited home turned out to be quite a good piano-player my battle was lost. This Welsh soldier was a favourite guest and after supper used to please my mother and father with his performances of Ketelby's 'In a Monastery Garden' and 'In a Persian Market'. The different sounds he coaxed out of that uncharitable instrument provoked a neighbour into saying in the morning: "Got a new piano then, missus?"

My unexpected companion went to get our glasses refilled, on one condition: "you don't mention my name in any of your books!" Although I assured him that I would say nothing remotely defamatory or embarrassing, he still insisted, and I was still thirsty, so we agreed.

When he returned to the window seat he introduced another surprising and forgotten subject. "We used to be rival delivery boys too, once, do you remember? We were butcher-boys, or, as one of my old customers used to call us, Meat Missionaries because we made her meagre rations feel like charity."

"But we needed the money, five bob a day from eight in the morning until six at night, biking in all weathers, greeted by grumbling customers and hostile dogs."

"I liked going to all the houses myself, they were all so different, especially when you were asked inside while the customers searched high and low for the money they'd 'put somewhere to be safe'."

I thought of some of those houses, each with their own particular smell. Some smelt of pipe-smoke and Brasso, some of dry-rot and mothballs, some of babies and cooking, some of rain and geraniums. Week after week you grew accustomed to the smells and sights of each house, the cupboards, boxes, pantries, crockery, sinks, calendars, pictures, plants, furniture, coal-buckets and cats.

"One woman was always having a bath when I called," I said, remembering the house with some amusement. "Like us, she only had a long zinc bath which she arranged in her kitchen for her weekly scrub. I always whistled louder as I approached the house, just to warn her . . ."

I knocked on the door.

" Who's that?"

" Butcher!"

" Come on in, love . . . dead on time again . . . you'll find a plate in that cupboard over there . . . that's right, the blue one that's chipped . . . and pass me some more soap while you're there, will you, me duck? Ta! . . . You'll find the money on the draining-board as usual . . ."

I always tried to appear casual and unimpressed, as if I found every customer naked in her bath when I called. She smiled at me as I clumsily wrote in my notebook that she'd paid.

" You good at sums?"

" Not bad . . . I'm better at spelling."

" Mucky stuff, money; you never know where it's been, do you . . . ?"

Every Saturday she rubbed her attractive body vigorously with the new bar of soap I'd given her and say: " I dunno, this blessed old war-time soap don't lather like it should, does it? Look, there's not enough damn bubbles here to make yourself decent . . ."

I smiled some sort of agreement, picked up my enamel tray and said, " Well, see you next week then!"

" Any time, darling . . . and tell that boss of yours not to send so much gristle next time or I'll be down to the shop and do him."

I promised to give him the message and strolled lamely out of her kitchen with a nonchalant cheerio that must have sounded more like the croak of a giraffe with laryngitis. When I eventually got on to my bike my legs kept missing the pedals and the fen country was seen through very bloodshot eyes for the next few minutes . . .

My friend said, " Now you can see why we were rivals, I never had that sort of luck. My most outstanding customer was an old bloke who lived in a bungalow where you never bothered to wipe your feet on the doormat going in because your shoes were alway dirtier coming out. This particular customer kept chickens in his bedroom because his neighbours objected to the smell in the garden. One Saturday when I called, the old man was ill in bed and his wife was out shopping . . ."

I knocked at the door.

" Come on in and make yourself at 'um."

I found my way into his bedroom and the first thing I saw was a magnificent cockerel sitting on the brass rail at the foot of the bed. It was a beautiful bird and sat there like an Egyptian Pharaoh.

" I can see you like my old cockerel," said the man. " Sits there all day long, he does, the lazy old devil . . . just staring like a vulture. He's a lovely critter though . . . you feel his crop . . . go on, he won't bite yer."

" What happens to him at night?"

" He stays where 'e is. The missis ain't too fond on him but it's company for me . . . anything's company when you're old . . ."

A few weeks later the customer died. It happened one Friday afternoon and when I made my usual Saturday morning call the old boy's wife insisted that I should go through to see him.

The blinds were drawn. The room was in semi-darkness. A jug and wash-basin stood on the table and a half-full chamber-pot with broken handle was still on the chest of drawers. When I looked at the bed all I could see was the thin, blind, stone face of the old man, no longer laughing or excited, but barren and expressionless, his bald head like a pebble in the sand of his soiled pillow. I looked at the foot of the bed and then at the old lady.

" Where's the cockerel?" I asked.

" He's gone too," she said in a flat, parched voice. " I wrung 'is neck last night and buried him in the garden near the rhubarb . . . I couldn't 'er stayed 'ere with 'im still alive, or eaten him. No, bless you. He was too much the other 'alf of Arthur, 'e was . . . no, they both had to go . . . it was only proper."

And then she began to cry and I withdrew from the room thinking, rather callously I suppose, what would have happened if the cockerel had died first . . .

We both smiled at the story and wondered for whom the bell had tolled earlier in the day when we'd stood on the bridge.

" Another drink?"

" No thanks."

*   *   *

We left the pub and walked back into the town. Many of the other pubs we'd remembered had disappeared. The school we'd attended was no longer a school. The cinema had gone, and so too were many of the people we had known and talked about. The houses where we had each been born, and the family butchers for whom we'd worked had also gone, and by the time we reached the Market Place we realized we were only on the scent of summer shadows that no longer had substance.

We parted at the Buttercross, saying over and over again how much we'd enjoyed a couple of hours together. One middle-aged man had brought back a gang of boys of the same class and time—Alan, Ernie, Ivan, Ted, Keith, Nigel, Jack and Frank, and if those summers were really anything like the way we'd remembered them then they were very special.

I felt tired and walked into the nearby churchyard to find a seat, my mind still busy trying to define some of those faint and undeciphered memories that were hidden in the skull like faded wall-paintings or half-finished cave drawings. From those jumbled frescoes of thirty-five years ago I recovered one memory I wished we had talked about and that was of Amy the Land Army girl we had both fallen in love with before we became butcher-boys. I think in the end I won Amy's affections because she used to take me with her on Saturday mornings delivering milk. Blonde, bright-eyed and witty, she seemed to enjoy every moment of her new life in rural surroundings. Her complexion already had a healthy tinge of early-morning freshness and her teeth were as white as peppermints.

I usually met her at the dairy in Station Road and we would start off by delivering milk to nearby houses and then make our way to the Market Place and on into High Street where there was a baker's shop at which we always stopped to buy a bag of cream buns. I don't remember ever doing enough work to earn such a feast but it was a feature of my Saturday mornings for many months.

Sometimes, and especially during school holidays, Amy would take me with her to one of the fields to milk the cows. As we opened the gate they would look up from their grazing and come slowly and automatically to be milked. I watched Amy's hands working rhythmically at the full udders, squeezing the soft teats that squirted warm, fresh milk into her metal pails.

She called it bell-ringing and once asked me to try. I did, but my nervous and uncertain hands only produced a few irregular trickles of milk that missed the pail and caused the cow to moo loudly with dissatisfaction. Amy laughed and said: " Fancy a country boy like you not knowing how to milk, and I come from the city where they think it grows in bottles."

The one thing I could do properly was fill the water-trough and on very hot afternoons the cattle crowded round me to get a drink of the cool, clean water. Their big eyes stared at me with dreamy, unthinking sadness, reflecting both the new shimmering water and the blue meadow of sky. I could have spent my whole life in that field. It was Eden all over again. As Thomas Traherne had written 240 years earlier:

All things were spotless and pure and glorious: yea, and infinitely mine, and joyful and precious. I know not that there were any sins, or complaints, or laws. I dreamed not of poverties, contentions or vices. All tears and quarrels were hidden from mine eyes . . . I saw all in the peace of Eden; heaven and earth did sing my Creator's praises, and could not make more melody to Adam, than to me. All Time was eternity . . . The skies were mine, and so were the sun and moon and stars, and all the world was mine, and I the only spectator and enjoyer of it . . .

Well, I had Amy to share it with; it was all Amy's and mine and I could not think that there was a war on, or that Hitler threatened to take this Eden from me. The scent of summer blossom from the hedgerows drifted like a pale gossamer cloud over the fields, softening the outlines of trees, making the landscape into a living water-colour. We sat there chewing our stalk of grass and listening to the skylarks without a care in the world. Once we were so struck by the loud trilling of the skylarks that we counted them. There were seventeen, all airborne and singing as if they were intent on bursting their quivering bodies.

" Have you noticed," said Amy, " that they're all facing the same way and singing into the wind! I wonder why?"

Her day's work done, Amy would lift her pails of milk on to the handle-bars of her bike and go back to the dairy. I left her then and biked back to my own street, to the rows of houses, the swifts and martins, the small warm rooms, and the waiting piano.

*   *   *

I slept for about three-quarters of an hour under a very warm
sun and was eventually woken up by a group of small girls
playing hopscotch at the other end of the path. The children
had returned from the trees and were singing their own times
and childhood into memory.

I wonder what fantasies they will be weaving into their talk
in thirty-five years' time? Will these summers too be the best
that were ever lived?

I leave my home town and drive back to the city along the
north bank of the Nene. The river is high and water laps at the
grassy bank. It was along this stretch of river that the fourteen-
year-old John Clare made his way by Dutch canal boat from
Peterborough to Wisbech in 1807 when he was seeking a job as
a junior clerk in a solicitor's office. He recalls the journey in his
autobiography:

> I started for Wisbeach with a timid sort of pleasure & when I got
> to Glinton turnpike I turned back to look on the old church as if I
> was going into another country. Wisbeach was a foreign land to
> me for I had never been above eight miles from home in my life . . .
> At Peterborough Brig I got into the boat that carrys passengers to
> Wisbeach once a week & returns the third day, a distance of
> twenty-one miles for eighteenpence . . .

Clare had been invited to Wisbech by his uncle Morris
Stimson who was footman to Councillor Bellamy, a local
solicitor in need of a young clerk. Stimson believed his young
nephew to be well suited to the post and had been over to
Helpston a week before to arrange for Clare to make the
journey to Wisbech.

> My mother trimmed me up as smart as she could, she found me a
> white neckcloth & got me a pair of gloves to hide my coarse hands
> But I had outgrown my coat & almost left my sleeves at the elbows
> & all my other garments betrayed too old an acquaintance with
> me to make me as genteel as could have been wished . . .

When the boat finally reached Wisbech Clare looked out
with the other passengers at the bridge that crossed the River
Nene and prepared to disembark. By this time the young poet
was quite sure he did not wish to become a solicitor's clerk, or

want to leave home. The speech he had prepared for Councillor Bellamy he promptly forgot and was so bewildered he did not even know where to start looking for the address.

> I was puzzled what to do & wished myself a thousand times over in my old corner at home At length my hand trembled & pulled the bell & to my great satisfaction my uncle came being the only manservant . . . said he " You must not hang your head but look up boldly & tell him what you can do "—so I went into the kitchen as bold as I could & sat down to tea. But I ate nothing . . . At length the Councillor appeard & I held my head as well as I could but it was like my hat almost under my arm. " Aye aye, so this is your nephew, Morris, is he . . ." " Yes Sir," said my uncle. " Well I shall see him again . . .

And he left the room rubbing his hands and never saw John Clare again. Clare was not all that disappointed for he thought that he " cut but a poor figure for a lawyer's clerk " and he spent the rest of the time looking round the shops of Wisbech until Sunday morning when the boat returned to Peterborough and he walked back to his parents' cottage in Helpston.

My journey back to the city is a little quicker and as I drive through the Norman gateway into the cathedral precincts I am reminded of another episode in Clare's life when he was befriended by Mrs Marsh, the Bishop of Peterborough's wife.

By this time Clare had published *Poems Descriptive of Rural Life and Scenery* in 1820 and Mrs Marsh was taking a great interest in the Helpston poet, having already persuaded her husband, the Right Reverend Dr Herbert Marsh, to deliver half a dozen bottles of port to the poet's poor cottage and give him an episcopal blessing.

The occasion of which I am thinking especially is recorded in Frederick Martin's *Life of John Clare*, published in 1865 only a year after Clare's death. It is an enchanting, colourful, and at times inaccurate account of the poet's life which has an immediacy and contact which other biographies lack. Martin was, after all, able to meet Clare's widow and acquaintances and to write about the places and landscape as Clare would have known them. His style can be extravagant but it is *alive*:

> The wife of the Right Reverend Dr. Herbert Marsh, an elderly lady of much energy, often felt lonesome in her old mansion at the foot of the big cathedral, for which suffering neither the sound

doctrinal sermons of her husband nor the saintly gossip of weekly tea-parties offered any remedy. There was a little theatre at the episcopal city, at which performances were given now and then; but the histrionic talent of the strolling players being of the slightest . . . the lady often felt time hanging heavy on her hands. In this exigency, Mrs. Marsh heard of the Helpston poet, and lost no time in making his acquaintance. Her kindly help and sympathy during his illness was greatly appreciated by Clare.

For a long time Clare refused the invitations to visit Mrs Marsh at the Bishop's Palace for he had experienced more than a few unpleasant encounters with clergymen—one of whom doubted Clare's authorship of the poems.

But pressed again and again to pay a short visit to Peterborough, Clare at length consented, being told that Dr. Marsh would be ' kept in his proper place ' and not allowed to interfere with him . . . Mrs. Marsh rejoiced that her poet had come at last and at once installed him in a funereal chamber overlooking the gardens . . . Before being led to this room Clare was informed by the lady that he would find several reams of paper, with stores of pens and ink for his poetic use, and would be at liberty to write anything he liked—epics, madrigals, pastorals, sonnets and even tragedies . . .

Poor Clare! The poet who could only compose in the fields, who loved the open air, who needed trees, birds and animals for companionship, was suddenly imprisoned by the kindest of motives and expected to write in a strange and very alien environment. It's no ordinary transition from a farm-labourer's cottage to a Bishop's Palace and Clare, understandably, felt miserable. The man who loved solitude was suddenly afraid of the stony silence and the orders that Mrs Marsh had given to her servants that he must be left alone. Clare wanted a drink and decided to escape.

So he marched down a final pair of stairs and through a small door out into the garden. There was a porter at the outer garden gate; but he too bowed in silence, and in another minute Clare found himself in the streets of Peterborough. The doors of the " Red Lion " stood hospitably open, and feeling starved, he went in to get some refreshments . . . Not having tasted any alcoholic drink for a long time, the ale produced a sort of stupefaction from which he did not recover until late in the day . . .

By this time Mrs Marsh had discovered that her bard had flown and sent her messengers to scour the city. They found him, eventually, at the inn and took him back to their mistress, who, rather charitably, assumed Clare's condition was due " to high poetic musings ". You can't get away with that kind of excuse today! Her only regret was that the supply of paper and ink had not been used up and she then persuaded Clare to go to bed early in preparation for a " day of great importance ". When he discovered that this was to be an afternoon tea-party to which all the local notabilities, the Dean, Archdeacons and Canons, had been invited, Clare shuddered and planned another escape.

> Once more he made his way down the broad flight of stairs . . . and a minute after stood in the High Street, opposite the Angel Inn. The coach for London, he was told, would start in half an hour. Clare took his seat, hid his face, as best as he could under a handkerchief . . . It was late at night when the Peterborough coach discharged its passengers at the " Bell and Crown " in Holborn . . .

Mrs Marsh again forgave Clare for disappearing for, several months later, when he was walking through the precincts she saw him and invited him to stay with her at the palace and accompany them one night to the theatre. Clare accepted and, on his last evening with her, went to see a performance of *The Merchant of Venice*.

Clare's behaviour at that performance is another story and very much connected with his increasing mental illness. He had left his " old home of homes " at Helpston and was now living at Northborough. He was only a year or two away from being sent to the General Lunatic Asylum at Northampton where he was to spend the last twenty-two years of his life.

It was at the village of Northborough that Clare's family grew and died. In fact, five of his children were to die before him and his wife was later to be buried with them in the cold and shaded east corner of the village churchyard. It is a sad and moving experience to stand there on any day among the grass, dandelions and nettles and to read the fading name of CLARE so many times.

I have on the wall above me an engraving of a cathedral done in 1827 and dedicated to " The Right Revd Herbert

Marsh, D.D; Lord Bishop of Peterborough ". On another wall
is a photograph of John Clare. They make an odd alliance, and
yet between the two I feel they give me a real link with their
times.

It is not the rejection or the neglect of this fine landscape
poet that haunts me, it is his loneliness, his sense of isolation,
brought about as much by his social status as his literary
genius. People tried to help, but in the wrong way and often for
the wrong reasons. Even the new cottage at Northborough was
not the answer. The loneliness was already too deep, the
despair too dark. I stood there the other day and tried to
imagine his feelings.

> They have brought me to a new house
> with larger grounds and a small rent,
> believing that song needs no more
> than a warm hearth or a field with a cow.
> But since she whom I love is no longer here
> how can my heart sing or a pen give wings
> to the sick bird in my breast? Song needs more
> than five acres of land and a thatched roof.
>
> The fields too are bare of the flowers
> I knew on Emmonsail Heath; the stream
> limps with its burden of cloud thro' the dark fen.
> Charity does not beget song,
> nor do the good intentions of those
> who know better the comforts of wealth.
> Without love, walls can only be walls,
> and the nightingale dead.

I have not heard a nightingale in the precincts but we do
have an owl nearby in the Bishop's garden, calling from trees
under which John Clare must have walked, and I listen to its
furry fluting late into the night, believing that its soft cry has
echoed out over the centuries, linking us all together in the
starry silence.

12

Tales of the Early Riser

" All you have to do," said John Lewis of Godmanchester, " is save your strength, sharpen up your perceptive abilities and get over here."

This was in reply to an ' early-warning' letter from me explaining that if I accepted his invitation to spend a few days with him on his boat on the Great Ouse he would be taking on the most incompetent, unpractical and useless member of his crew.

The invitation, however, grew in my mind to become something of a challenge and so here I am, making my way over the fens to the Lewises' Bookshop—and their boat—in Godmanchester. I'm still wondering if I have saved up enough strength or sharpened up my perceptive abilities sufficiently to take in a wholly new experience.

I first met John and his wife Doreen a few weeks ago when they asked me if I would give a reading for them in the lovely old barn at the rear of the shop. I shared the evening (which was in aid of the Arthritis and Rheumatism Council) with the Cambridge poet Heather Buck and we were delighted to find an audience of over a hundred waiting to receive us.

The evening was very warm. The air smelt of wine and strawberries—which were to be served during the interval— and there was a ' sense of occasion' about the place as we began. An audience can lift you or deflate you, it can inspire or destroy. We were lucky. Our audience responded quickly and encouraged us to try the heights.

When the first half was over we all went down into the garden and strolled about under the trees or down to the river. The garden was full of golden light as the sun began to set and the wine glistened in our glasses, as if the sunlight itself had been bottled and served specially for the evening.

The wine and strawberries over, we returned to the barn for the second half of the reading and, as the light faded and cooler air flowed in through open windows, I could not imagine a happier way of spending a Saturday night in summer.

Later, a few of us stayed to have supper with John, Doreen, and their family, and the talk went on into the early hours of morning. It was then that John suggested that I ought to take a look at the Cambridgeshire countryside from the river. I grasped at the suggestion and a date was fixed.

That date has now arrived and I begin to hurry towards my destination, hoping that the weather will hold good for just a few more days. It has been warm all week but the egg-shell blue sky is getting a cooler look about it; the wind has changed to the north. The early evening light changes to silver and the clouds of burnt sienna have undertones of deep grey.

The streets of Huntingdon are already deserted. The shops closed, the shoppers and office-workers gone home. It's as quiet now as William Cowper must have known it, or William Cobbett when he praised its " beautiful meadows ".

As I drive into Godmanchester I realize again what an attractive place it is, particularly in the evening with the low light of the sun on the houses and the heavy traffic finished for another day. It has, despite all the changes around Huntingdon in recent years, managed to retain much of its character, particularly on the riverside. Its history goes back to before Roman times and it remained a place of some importance right through the Middle Ages until the nineteenth century. As late as the seventeenth century it was still being referred to as " a very great country Toune ".

Among the town's records are preserved early charters, including the first which was given by King John in 1214 and which converted the town into a self-governing manor; a rare distinction then but now no more. For the privilege bestowed upon them by His Majesty the townspeople agreed to pay £120 each year to the King and his successors. Honours are all very well, but they can be expensive.

There are several fine houses in Godmanchester, including some half-timbered, and there is a small Elizabethan grammar school, still in use, though not as a grammar school but, at present, a private nursery school where the children sound more contented and relaxed than the original pupils.

One of the most popular features of the place today is the Chippendale-Chinese Bridge, built in 1827, which crosses the river like a starched white lace collar. It must be the most photographed bridge in the area, outside Cambridge of course, and it is indeed very pleasant to stand on it for a while and look across the water to the old houses.

Its character and appeal do not diminish with familiarity, and certainly as I drive up to the bookshop now I appreciate more than ever the quality of dignified calm that Godmanchester manages to preserve.

Within minutes I am on the boat with no time for second thoughts or excuses.

"We shan't get very far this evening," says John, "but it will give us a much better start in the morning."

The boat rocks gently as the last few provisions are stowed on board. I notice that the name of the vessel is *Early Riser* and imagine myself being shaken out of my sleeping-bag at 4 a.m.

Doreen, and one of her daughters, look partly relieved and partly worried as they wave goodbye—an encouraging farewell that also says "they'll never make it".

This trip is something of an experiment for the three of us who have finally made it—John Lewis himself, Rod Stratford and me. It's the first time the three of us have been together, we're not sure how far we're going, or what we are doing, beyond the vague notion of having a few days on the river for my sake, and for this book. If it's a disaster, that's one chapter less. I look at my notebooks and their empty pages. Shall I get anything written by the time we return? Forget the book, I tell myself, and enjoy the trip.

The evening is calm with the faintest sliver of a new moon just visible between the clouds. I first see it over my right shoulder, which is supposed to be lucky. And I'm not looking at it through glass, which is supposed to be unlucky. The superstitions are comforting.

As we cruise slowly through the dark green water towards the first lock. I feel that I already belong to a different world, a world that does not belong to the land, or the land's routine.

"You'll have a totally different concept of time, too," says John. "Two days on the water feel as long as a week.

Everything is so much slower. Sometimes you get delays. You have to learn how to wait and be patient. But it's all part of the life, all part of the unwinding."

By the time we are through the Godmanchester Lock the mist is rising over the water-meadows, the largest publicly-owned meadows in the country. The sky deepens into a striking piebald pattern of orange and brown. The riverside darkens. Chestnut and willow trees are no more than shadows. The boat moves slowly downstream into a kind of mystery.

As we pass under the bridge connecting Huntingdon and Godmanchester there is a strong feeling of history, as if going under bridges rather than over them is now a much better way of appreciating the past. When this bridge was built, construction started from both banks and legend has it that when it was finished it didn't quite meet in the middle. Well it does now, and you'd need better light than this to see the join! They were not the last builders to have that problem and I seem to remember something very similar happening to a new bridge that was built in the fens a few years ago.

The curl of moon drifts clear of cloud. A heron rises from the bank and crosses the bow of the boat once or twice in what appears to be a display of protest. In the twilight its wings look enormous, prehistoric, a resurrection from a million years' sleep.

Time has already lost its meaning. The evening darkens totally. On our port side the lighted church of All Saints at Hartford suddenly appears through the trees. It could not look more attractive on Christmas Eve. Further on the pinhead lights of small boats already moored for the night perforate the riverbank. Water and meadows become one. John decides it is time for us to moor for the night too, and brings the boat gently into the bank.

The engine stops. The boat is secured. Only the water laps softly at the side; otherwise stillness. The words of Walt Whitman come to mind.

> Out of the cradle endlessly rocking . . .
> Out of the ninth-month midnight.

The three of us agree that the air is cool enough for a brandy before supper. Its warmth prepares us nicely for the delicious meal of Grafham trout that Doreen has thoughtfully put on board for us.

So we have got this far and will, I'm sure, survive the first night. It's not the end of the world, admittedly, but water can give you such a feeling of separation. And after the pressures of the last few weeks it's a good feeling. We talk through the next three hours and, for all we know, could be becalmed in the Pacific Ocean, certainly not within walking distance of home.

Contentment. Tiredness. Sleep. That's all I remember. When I wake in the cold, early morning light I have lost track of time and dates. I dress and go for a walk before either John or Rod stir.

Cattle have come down from the field and now graze at the waterside or stare inquisitively at this newcomer. The sun rises behind layers of cloud, creating a streaky-bacon sky. The thought makes me feel hungry. The gulls' cries sound full of winter. There is a keenness in the early morning air that can almost be called arctic.

When I get back to the boat my hopes are realized. The frying-pan is on the stove. I can smell bacon cooking and tea is brewed.

Breakfast takes nearly as long as supper and it's another hour or more before we move slowly downstream to Houghton.

The meadows glow green even under a sunless sky and the swallows are busily skimming low over the grass for a last meal of insects before their big migration. What fascinating flight-weavers they are, and what remarkable navigators.

Houghton is an appealing little village with several well-kept houses and the very ancient Mill, which now belongs to the National Trust and is used as a youth hostel.

We have to wait quite a while to get through the Houghton Lock and decide to walk up to the village for a morning pint and a game of darts. Because we are not experts the competition is fierce to prove that we are. Somehow we each win a game, thus ensuring that the remainder of the trip continues harmoniously.

When we leave the pub we rejoice to see the sun shining and there is a brightness on the water as we return to the boat. It's amazing what a game of darts can do to the weather.

This is a very beautiful stretch of river; indeed, it is all the way from beyond Godmanchester almost to Earith. As we approach the Hemingfords I see what I have been looking for all morning—a kingfisher. Its plumage suddenly emerges from a bush to starboard and torpedoes over to port, a whirring, dazzling, little rocket of blue and green, shooting over the water to a broken branch opposite. It reminds me of the first kingfisher I ever saw when I was a child in a much warmer summer many years ago. Then I thought that what I had just seen was so beautiful it could not belong to earth. The excitement never leaves me. It makes me think too of an afternoon when I went to work with some children in a school near Bedford. When I asked them to describe a kingfisher, one little nine-year-old said " A kingfisher is a living rainbow." I can't beat that.

The Great Ouse is a good river for bird-watching. In a thick bed of reeds I can see two reed-bunting and the water is continually criss-crossed by martins and swallows. Ahead of us a kestrel hovers, almost motionless, with that remarkably poised stillness and control of flight. How appropriate that this bird should also be known as the windhover.

One thing I have discovered is that Hemingford Grey also has to be seen from the water to appreciate its full beauty. The old houses and gardens, the cottages and the church, all look particularly lovely from the river. The graffiti daubers haven't been able to leave the walls alone, of course, and are as thoughtless of other people's pleasure as are some of the casual boat-users who bully their way past at speed, with no thought for the true river-lovers or the erosion of the river-banks.

Sailing, or cruising, down a river is, I've realized, like reading the biography of a river; every bend, bank, lock and change of current becomes part of its character; the fields, colours, smells and wildlife add to its features.

The locks are, of course, a very important part of any river's life and on the Great Ouse there are fifteen locks between Bedford and Earith, all of which have to be maintained to protect the river and the land.

We pass under the ancient chapel-bridge of St Ives, noticing its two different styles of arches, and go placidly on towards Holywell. Here you can see the Ferry Boat Inn, which claims to be the oldest inn in England, having been in existence since 1066. It also claims to be haunted by the ghost of Juliet Tewsley who hanged herself on St Patrick's Day in 1050 after being jilted. Well, belief is everything and if anyone tells me they've seen the sad maiden I'll not contradict them.

The fan-shaped rays of the sun stretch out of a north-wind sky and the distant fields are illuminated for a few moments. Five hag-noisy rooks fly over the meadows, cackling and arguing about something, perhaps us. A wren on a nearby twig of willow takes no notice but goes about her own fussy business.

There is always something to take your attention, some building, tree, bird, boat or animal. The Great Ouse also has its share of good riverside inns—like the Ferry Boat, the Pike and Eel, and the Fish and Duck—but as tempting as some of them are we stay on board, at least for the time being. After all, we're not doing too badly. John is a pretty good cook, the food is three-star and the beverages plentiful. Rod Stratford has perfected a particularly good drink for keeping out the cold. It began as sweet coffee with a dash of brandy but I think he has experimented quite a bit and has now got the measure about right—fifty-fifty. We begin to call it the Ouse Cocktail, but decide it ought to be named after the boat, so an ' Early Riser ' is, for me, no longer just a boat or an American prune, but also a special chest-warming drink that's very good at keeping out the damp and the north wind. I can't help having the thought, however, that if this is what we need in summer, what would we need in winter? Even the ' old salts ' admit it's cold and, as well as the Early-Riser coffees, we keep brewing pots of gunpowder green tea.

I mentioned a moment ago the importance of the lock system on the river and we have several to thread our way through, some manually operated, some electrically operated. The one at Brownshill Staunch is worked by a young lock-keeper and his wife—Nigel and Trisha Dummett, who have happily and sensibly decided to live the kind of life they want to live by turning their backs on comfortable indoor jobs with superannuations at the end of forty years' boredom. Instead of going for the glossy life promised by the advertisements, instead of trying to keep up with everybody else and enduring the city life they had, they now live in an isolated cottage lodged between the river bank and the flat, open fields of Cambridgeshire. They grow their own vegetables, make their own beer, enjoy plenty of fresh air and the company of passing travellers like ourselves. During the summer season they see over one hundred boats a day through the lock, with many more at holiday weekends.

" But what of the winter?" I ask, feeling the cynicism of middle-age blunting the romantic in me.

" Ah, then we shall be able to have plenty of time to ourselves, and when it gets dark we shall cuddle up by the fire with a glass of home-brew and listen to music for hours," says Trisha, with the shining eyes of a child on Christmas morning.

They guide us through the lock with such charm and friendliness that we are already looking forward to meeting them again on our return.

" It's been a pleasure to help you through the lock," says Trisha. " Have a good trip."

" Keep sober," says Nigel, as he enters us in his log.

We are sailing now through a land of white willows and reed-beds, through a country of wind and wildfowl. Rod has gone to sleep.

" Take the wheel," says John. " I'll make some more tea."

And to my delight and astonishment I find myself at the helm, not only of the *Early Riser* but also of the *Cutty Sark*. Immediately my Walter Mitty complex takes over. I become Humphrey Bogart in *The African Queen* or Gregory Peck in *Moby Dick*. The grey ripple of the Ouse is a cauldron of shark-filled seas and the willow plantation is a jungle. Where are the whales? Where are the headhunters?

" Keep it steady!" shouts John from the galley.

" Aye-aye, skipper!"

*   *   *

In the flatter, more open country on the edge of the fens the wind comes at us with more force and the boat sways. We are making now for Twentypence Inn and the Old West River, where we have decided to moor for the night.

In the distance I can see the last of the corn stubble fires and the great patches of charred earth where the fields have already been burnt. There is something so final and ritualistic about it, as though the fires declare the end of summer, the death of a season, the ashes of harvest. These fires are, in Emily Dickinson's words, like the " far ends of tired days " and they stir the imagination.

Far off,
like secret camp-fires burning in the night,
patches of blazing cornstalk break the dark,
singeing the shallow mist with streaks of smoke.

Cut off
from all the cold machinery of day
those flames could be the centre of deep thought,
of soldiers' plans and ancient heraldry.

Night waits
The nostrils sniff again the earth-charred air
until from this quiet ridge above the fields
the mind hears bugles calling in the wind.

It is dark by the time we secure the boat and John goes off to
the inn to phone his wife, to let her know that we have at least
made it this far.

We then discover that a great treat is in store for us. Doreen
and her daughters are on their way with a complete dinner of
home-made pâté, roast turkey, vegetables, cheese and wine. In
about three-quarters of an hour there are seven of us sitting in
the small cabin of the *Early Riser* having a feast that few
kitchens could have equalled. We rock, we glow, we eat. It only
needs a decorated barge of musicians to float by now playing
music specially composed for the occasion by a Mr George
Frederick Handel and we shall feel . . . but here goes Walter
Mitty again with his claret-coloured fantasies. It must be the
cold and this different concept of time that John warned me
about, hours, days, or weeks ago.

The meal is over. The ladies leave to return to Godmanchester. The well-fed crew decide to call it a night. It's been
a long, eventful day. Now all we need is sleep, Keats's " soft
embalmer of the still midnight . . ."

It shouldn't be difficult. We take a short walk along the bank
and nearly fall down a twelve-foot precipice as, in the pitch
dark, we come to a slipway that has just been cut through the
bank to a new marina which is in the early stages of construction. We were, literally, only one step and one second
from disaster because I don't think we should have got up
again. How we stopped in time I shall never know. It
convinced me that there *are* such things as guardian angels—
and very understanding ones too.

*   *   *

I wake very early. Two cockerels are crowing to each other across the hidden countryside in the dawn's grey light. I listen to them for nearly half an hour and then their calls are joined by those of wild ducks.

John and Rod are still asleep so I slip out through the hatch to avoid disturbing them and walk downstream to where the Old West slinks like a sidewinder through the grass.

This stretch of the original River Ouse's course is a much quieter part of the fenland waterways since Vermuyden cut the Bedford rivers from Earith to Denver and it's difficult now to imagine that these untroubled waters once knew the fury of winter floods.

The water is perfectly still and marble-patterned with the reflection of clouds. The morning air already begins to smell of autumn. It polishes your face with its invisible roughness like a clean towel.

It has a keenness about it that reminds you of those old films of pioneering days when the homesteaders broke the ice on the water troughs before they could wash the sleep out of their eyes. It's an earthy, primitive moment to be out in the world, away from cars, telephones, rush and noise.

I watch a family of reed-bunting on the opposite bank. A coal-tit settles on a nearby hawthorn bush. The sky grows brighter. The only sound is of the cattle again, snatching at grass or splashing their pancakes of wet dung on to the ground.

I walk for about a mile before turning back. Once again I feel ready for breakfast. I hope John is up and coaxing the same delicious smell out of that old frying-pan. He is.

*   *   *

Beyond Twentypence Bridge the Old West continues to flow calmly down to Stretham where, beyond the wooden bridge, is the now well-known Stretham Engine—a Boulton and Watt beam engine which was kept in use for a hundred years from 1831 and is still in working order. It is a museum piece of special fascination to anyone interested in machines or the history of fen drainage. The engine-house is open to the public and is worth breaking the journey for, whether by road or water.

Just beyond Stretham is Pope's Corner where the Old West joins up with the River Cam. Here you have the choice of going to Cambridge or continuing to Ely; neither destination is comfortably within our reach on this particular trip and, with a quick look at the deteriorating weather, we decide to head for home.

For those who can linger longer in these waters it is also worth mentioning that you are not far from Wicken Fen Nature Reserve, should you feel like trying your legs on land for a change.

We have another five hours before us and are beginning to feel ready for a good hot bath. The north wind freshens. Squally showers blow across the fens. Rod is kept busy with supplies of ' Early-Risers ' and the conversation lapses into long periods of reflection.

An R.A.F. bomber flies low overhead but is hardly visible through the heavy clouds. It is a reminder of how busy these skies once were during the Second World War when several British and American squadrons were based in the county and set off across the fens for bombing raids on Germany. Several of the deserted airstrips can still be seen, overgrown with thistles and weeds, the empty huts and control towers ghostly with memories. Some, of course, are still in use as air-bases for today's fighting forces. The modern jets have not obliterated the nostalgia of some old airmen for the Lancasters and Super Fortresses they used to fly. They still return to relive " the greatest time of your life, if you survived ".

* * *

We arrive once more at Brownshill Staunch and as we're the only boat wanting to go through the lock at the moment we have to call at the lock-keeper's house to let them know we're around.

The more I think about it the more I admire Nigel and Trisha for wanting to do this kind of job. You need more than a pleasant disposition and a few hundred records. You also need a strong character and faith in each other. They have however, dispelled my cynicism and made me a romantic again. The vegetables look healthy. The home-brew promises to be good. There are stacks of records to hear and books to be read before an open fire, and " there's always the river for company ".

They come with us up to the lock and stay talking with us for quite some time. We invite them to have one of Rod's 'special coffees' with us, which they agree is pretty good, and they learn as much about each of us as we learn about them. A tremendous warmth encircles us as we stand grouped there like climbers who have just conquered Everest. The vibrations make a bright halo of unspoken words. There is a quietness in the air that no cold wind or rain can destroy.

As the boat drifts away from the lock we look back and wave. We know that the lock-keeper and his wife will survive the winter all right and not regret one moment of it.

And so back to Holywell, St Ives, Hemingford Grey, Houghton, Hartford, Huntingdon and Godmanchester. Birds and trees are once again no more than shadows. The lights of cottage windows glint like fallen stars across the water. We are ready for home, for landfall and warmth.

By the time we moor the boat and unload it is dark and we are weary. We feel as if we have been on the water for a month. When we walk into the house a cooked supper is waiting for us—a spicy Balkan dish that turns our iceberg bodies into braziers.

Afterwards there is only one thing we long for—sleep! But sleep is not so easy back on land. I feel myself still rocking and when I open my eyes I am alarmed to find myself stationary whilst the room is swinging backwards and forwards. When I close my eyes again my mind is active with all that it has received during the past three days. Kingfishers startle my dreams. Willow trees drown me in their pools of silvery grey. Herons haunt. Boats nudge me to the edge of the bed and the carpet reflects white clouds. I sigh and steer my bed into Brownshill Staunch lock and a smiling young couple say "Look who we've got here!" And I cry to the crescent moon,

"Throw me back into the dream-giddy water; let me drown in its laughing and shining dark."

If there is any Celtic blood in my veins—as some people assure me there is—then my ancestral spirit says, "Oh it was a lovely weekend, lovely!" And I do agree.

*　　*　　*

This thought of ancestry again teases my mind. How deep down do the roots go? How far back can the blood's rhythm be traced? Do we belong to a particular place, or a special tribe?

Why do we feel happier and more contented in some places than others? The only other part of the country where I feel nearly as *at home* as I do in the fens is Wales. The two landscapes and the two races of people could not be more different and yet I find myself having a deep affinity with both. I tell myself I am a fenman through and through, the product of several generations of fenmen, and I know where I find the greatest satisfaction, the greatest contentment, the most satisfying feeling of being among my own folk.

I would go back now to the axe-ring
and the aching round in the wood's being;
footstep and armstroke in the daily need
of fire and shelter. Should this be denied
in the last hours I would lose all that the blood
has journeyed for; bruised by the cold winds
of a love's winter a worn man should be
where the roots are, where the tree-rings
are those of his father's father; and when eyes close
sweet music should come, like the smell of wood
to the wood-cutter's nostrils, to comfort his soul.

Of all things that call me back to the tribe's ground,
to the grip of tongues and primitive sounds
providing fire, it is the rhythm of songs sung
in the feeble light of a family evening
when questions brood on familiar faces.
A man knows then when his ambitions have faded,
when women fail to quicken the heart-beat and lust ceases.
Melody comes from the longings of man,
from the dreams that have drawn him, kept him
beyond mountains in an alien landscape,
studying stones more than stars for his horoscope.

I would go back to the rhythm of seasons and singing,
to the rhythm of axe-ring and labour,
of cradle and water, hearthside and harbour,
A man knows his landfall when the journey is over,
sees in the firelight the spent flames of the lover.
That plain girl with her straight hair, bringing
water in a chipped horn and her first bread,
is better by far than those silken women
in once-travelled kingdoms. The rhythm of sleep
and the rhythm of voices, these are the virtues
to prize when each weary eye closes.

13

To Travel Hopefully

Until a couple of years or so ago it was, I seem to remember, very unfashionable to spend your holidays at home, in your own country. After all, went the argument, what has Britain got to offer; you never know when the sun is going to shine, if at all. And the cost of everything—hotels, wine, cigarettes, car parks, entertainment; no duty-free shops; no sun-tan; no exotic labels to stick on your luggage. Then there's the language-barrier! Well, I mean, if you go abroad everybody can speak *English*, but if you go on holiday in Yorkshire, Wales, Norfolk, the Midlands, Liverpool or Glasgow, you can't understand half they say. Holidays at home? You must be joking! So the Costa Brava and Lucerne, Capri and Yugoslavia were the places to go to and it was not uncommon for English people to be familiar with villages in Italy or Greece but ignorant of the Cotswolds or Cumbria. I recently saw some geography examination papers and the answers completely redesigned the British Isles. The Pennines were switched to Scotland. The Isle of Wight was off the coast of Wales or near the North Sea oil-fields. Edinburgh had quietly slipped down into Yorkshire, without the Scots knowing, and the Wash had taken over the Bristol Channel.

George Borrow said it more succinctly in his Preface to *Lavengro*—" There are no countries in the world less known by the British than these self-same lands."

I'm not knocking overseas travel, far from it; I have enjoyed continental holidays myself and hope there will be more. Travel is, according to Francis Bacon, " for the young a part of education and for the old part of experience ". But I think it is also worth knowing your own country well too—and not just the obvious places. You may not get a Mediterranean sun-tan or a dog-eared passport but you may be surprised at what there is in this country apart from Blackpool, Brighton, Buxton or Bude.

I suppose we rightly consider ours to be the great age of travel, but it is so only because of the greater number of people who live now and can afford to fly, sail, leave home for weeks at a time and explore other continents. But men and women have always been travellers, adventurers, and explorers. You did not have to be a Columbus or Captain Cook, or a privileged person on the Grand Tour, to enjoy moving around, watching other people live and work.

In fact England was a tourist attraction long before America was discovered. Over 500 years ago Erasmus was writing from this country to his friends on the Continent urging them to cross the Channel.

> If you are wise, you too will fly over here. Did you but know the blessings of Britain, you would clap wings to your feet and run hither . . . wherever you go you are received on all hands with kisses . . . Oh, if you had once tasted how sweet and fragrant those kisses are, you would indeed wish to be a traveller—not for ten years but for your whole life in England.

Whatever happened to the English temperament? How did we become such a reserved and unemotional race of people after Erasmus's experience of us? Surely if we treated our visitors today with such fervour they would think we had gone out of our minds.

And talking of going out of our minds, Shakespeare seems to have had mixed views about England. In the graveyard scene in *Hamlet*, you will remember the dialogue that the Prince has with one of the clowns—

FIRST CLOWN: . . . it was that very day that young Hamlet was born: he that is mad and sent into England.

HAMLET: Ay, marry, why was he sent into England?

FIRST CLOWN: Why, because he was mad; he shall recover his wits there; or, if he do not, 'tis no great matter there.

HAMLET: Why?

FIRST CLOWN: 'Twill not be seen in him there; there the men are as mad as he.

In fairness to the bard he also wrote of England as " this other Eden, demi-paradise . . . this blessed plot " etc . . . and many other memorable tributes.

The seventeenth century produced a number of travel-writers and in 1639 Peter Mundy published *The Travels of Peter Mundy*. In that volume he makes it clear that the argument for ' home or away ' holidays is by no means a new one: " There is more to be enjoyed, more to be seen at home in our own land (take it in general) than in any one country besides in the whole world, both for conveniency and delight."

That may, or may not, be an exaggeration, but for its size Britain does have a considerable variety of riches. London, Cambridge, Oxford, Canterbury, York, Edinburgh, Bristol, Stratford, Chester, Devon, Cornwall, Norfolk, Wales, the Peak District, the Highlands, the Lake District, the coastline, the hills, farms, valleys and fens—all within an area smaller than some of the individual states of America.

What is so surprising about some of these early horse-riding tourists is the amount of distance they covered in one day—and the degree of discomfort they were prepared to tolerate. Let me quote Peter Mundy again.

Being now at Gloster, and Wales so near, I had a desire to see some of that country also, so took my journey thitherwards. First I went to Ross, then to Abergayney [sic]. Riding from thence, about a mile from the town my horse threw me into a deep dirty pool of water, over head and ears. At length I got up again, sore bruised against some stones that my sides met withal, and came to Llangroyna, a village where I was fain to pawn my sword for a little money to carry me back to Gloster . . .

He goes on to describe his visit the following day to Monmouth where he saw the ruins of the castle in which Henry V was born, and how he then went deeper into the mountains and valleys of Wales where the hostelries would certainly not have made the pages of some of today's guides. " My inn was none of the richest nor my hostess none of the youngest, being 108 years of age, stark blind, half deaf, with never a word of English . . . My bed was of good fresh straw on which I slept as well as feathers." I don't think Dickens could have created a more striking character than that ancient, stark, blind, half-deaf hostess of 108 years.

The seventeenth century also saw a lot of overseas visitors coming to this country and their observations are worth recalling. In 1610 a Swiss gentleman, writing home, had this to say: " Those who are desirous of visiting the entire kingdom hire interpreters, of whom there are many who make it a profession . . . Travellers usually go on horseback, sometimes in coaches, which are too dear."

In 1737 a Frenchman was advising his friends against coming to England, despite its beauties, for fear of being robbed.

> You have heard of the bad management in England with regard to the highways, and you know that here, as in Turkey and Persia, a man cannot travel without running the hazard of being robbed. Your friend, M.C., who arrived yesterday at Newmarket, was surprised last year near Cambridge by the celebrated Dick Turpin . . . The highwayman, after having repeated in vain the word of command to stand and deliver, in order to punish him for his disobedience, fired a pistol at him; but the ball happily missed.

So Dick Turpin wasn't such a crack shot after all. I bet he wouldn't have missed though if they made a film of that incident.

But not all the overseas visitors were robbed or disappointed. In 1782 a German schoolmaster was able to write:

> Yesterday I had the luxury for the first time of being driven in an English stage. These coaches are, at least in the eyes of a foreigner, quite elegant, lined in the inside; and with two seats large enough to accommodate six persons . . . I must observe that they have a curious way of riding not in, but upon a stage-coach. Persons to whom it is not convenient to pay a full price, instead of the inside, sit on the top of the coach, without seats or rails. By what means passengers thus fasten themselves securely on the roof, I do not know; but you constantly see numbers seated there, apparently at their ease and in perfect safety . . . in summer time, in fine weather, on account of the prospects it is certainly more pleasant without than it is within, excepting that the company is generally low.

So, you either enjoyed the fresh air and scenery with a load of ruffians, or you stayed with the genteel in a stuffy carriage and saw very little.

But was it as bad as that? In 1809 a Swedish visitor was much more impressed.

I arrived here the day before yesterday after a rapid journey from Yarmouth. How capitally one travels in England—superb horses, equipages with which one could cut a dash in Sweden's capital city; inns where a word procures every comfort . . . The country is cultivated and lovely beyond all description. I have never seen a more beautiful picture of industry. Mankind's intelligent dominion over nature is here so universal, so complete . . . Here is a richer vegetation. The grass has a colour, a density which delights the eye . . .

Had you but lived in the middle of the twentieth century, sir, you would have been invited over for a fortnight's holiday at our expense for such a generous testimonial.

But let us return for a moment to the seventeenth century and to a more famous writer and traveller—Samuel Pepys. His letters, diaries and journals are full of interesting observations, particularly about this county of Cambridgeshire and the fen country. On 17 September 1663 he wrote:

I was to come to a new consideration, whether it was fit to let my uncle and his son go to Wisbeach about my uncle Day's estate alone or no, and concluded it unfit. And so, leaving my wife I began a journey with them, and with much ado through the fens, along dykes, where we were ready to have our horses sink to the belly, we got by night, with a great deal of stir and hard riding, to Parson Drove, a heathen place, where I find my uncle and aunt Perkins and their daughters, poor wretches! in a sad, poor thatched cottage like a barn in a stable . . .

The contrast between this and his visits to Hinchingbrooke House is obvious and Pepys decided he could not stay with his relatives, so retired to the local inn for accommodation. Again, it was one not likely to win any rosettes from Mr Egon Ronay or the Tourist Board. " And so, about twelve at night or more, to bed in a sad, cold, nasty chamber . . . and so to sleep, but was cruelly bitten by gnats."

Within the week that followed, Pepys rode to Wisbech, Cambridge, Huntingdon, Brampton, Grafham, and back to London, coping with business matters, a sick wife, stolen horses, hot weather and several discomforts. That was certainly clocking up the mileage by one-horse-power standards.

Another intrepid traveller of those times was Celia Fiennes, a daughter of Colonel Nathaniel Fiennes, one of the Protector's favourite officers, whose daughter was clearly a very determined young lady, especially on a horse. She travelled the length and breadth of England, including the fens, and left a lively account of her impressions in *Journeys into Severall Parts of England*. Her style and spelling have a quaintness that needs getting used to, but there are rewards:

> Notwithstanding ye Cleaning of their parlour for me I was not able to beare the roome. The smell of hay was perfume, and I Rather Chose to stay and see my horse Eate their provender in the stable than to stand in yt roome, for I Could not bring myself to sit down. I Could have no stomach to Eate any of the ffood they should order, and finding they had noe wheaten bread I told my Landlady I could not Eate their Clapt out bread so I bought the ffish she got for me, wch was full Cheap Enough, nine pence for two pieces of Salmon halfe a one neer a yard long and a very Large trout of an amber Coullour . . .

There are always moments of amusement, at least to the reader, in some of these old travel writings. The poet John Dryden writing to a friend at Cotterstock, near Fotheringhay, on 23 November 1698, describes his journey to London by coach.

> My journey to London was yet more unpleasant than my abode at Tichmarsh; for the coach was crowded up with an old woman, fatter than any of my hostesses on the road. Her weight made the horses travel very heavily; but, to give them a breathing time, she would often stop us, and plead some necessity of Nature, and tell us we were all flesh and blood. But she did this so frequently that at last we conspired against her, and that she might not be inconvenienced by staying in the coach, turned her out in a very dirty place where she was to wade up to the ankles before she could reach the next hedge . . .

Poor woman! They wouldn't have done that to her on National Coaches or British Rail. But, in 1698, one can appreciate the annoyance she would have been to her fellow passengers. How difficult it must have been in those days to keep to timetables, or get to appointments punctually.

Such travelling, however, continued into the eighteenth century with people like Horace Walpole, Thomas Gray, Thomas Carlyle and James Boswell. Walpole was, I admit, always pining for an Italian inn when staying at an English one and if his experience at Wellingborough was repeated too often one can understand why.

We lay at Wellingborough—pray never lie there—the beastliest inn on earth is there! We were carried into a vast bedchamber, which I suppose is the clubroom, for it stunk of tobacco like a Justice of the Peace . . . Tomorrow we see Burleigh and Peterborough and lie at Ely; on Monday we hope to be back in town.

That was in 1793 and I'm sure—or am I?—that things would be different now. I imagine most of us have been offered hotel rooms that " Stunk of tobacco like a Justice of the Peace " but have never been able to describe it so eloquently.

Scotland was a great attraction to the hardy travellers of those days and the mileage covered by James Boswell and Samuel Johnson is quite staggering. They didn't get it all their own way, of course; the tide and the weather have made most travellers wait at some time or other on their journeys. In two or three hundred years' time people might find it very quaint that travellers in 1978 had to wait for hours at airports for flights that could not take off either because of bad weather or strikes, or some cock-up among the operators. For Samuel Johnson, in 1773, it was simply the weather.

> I am still confined in Skye. We were unskilful travellers and imagined that the sea was an open road which we could pass at pleasure; but we have now learned with some pain that we may still wait for a long time the caprices of the equinoctial winds, and sit reading or writing, as I do now, while the tempest is rolling the sea or roaring in the mountains . . .

When we come to the nineteenth-century travel-writers, we have that formidable, tantalizing, verbose, controversial but brilliant pen-man—William Cobbett. His *Rural Rides* is still a classic of observation, comment, good sense and awareness. I seem to have quoted Cobbett so often in this book that I will refrain from giving too much space to him here, but one passage from his *Autobiography* will show that his journeys were not always peaceful and his popularity not very strong amongst the establishment. He had already served a prison sentence in 1812 for his political activities and criticisms of the nation's economy, but his fight for " the labouring people and paupers of England " urged him back into politics and in 1820, " I resolved to stand for Parliament again."

I set off for Coventry with my eldest daughter on the 28th of February. We went all the night (the coldest of the winter) in a post-chaise; breakfasted at Daventry, and then proceeded on towards Dunchurch, which is eleven miles from Coventry. Here we were met by messengers who brought accounts that I should certainly be murdered if I attempted to enter the city. A band of rich ruffians had leagued together against me. They had got together a parcel of men, whom they made partly drunk, and whom they gave orders to go out, meet me at a bridge a mile from the city, and if I refused to return to London, to fling me over the bridge . . . On Wednesday morning the election began; and the poll closed in the afternoon, leaving me at the head of it. On Thursday, the savages came well fed and well supplied all the day long with gin and brandy, brought out to them in glass bottles . . . I, that day, saw about twenty of my voters actually torn away from the polling-place, and ripped up behind, and stripped of their coats. [As] I went out of the Booth I had to pass through bands of savages, and I was scarcely among them, when they began to endeavour to press me down. I got many blows in the sides and, if I had been either a short or weak man I would have been inevitably killed . . . One of the savages exclaimed " Damn him, I'll rip him up!" He was running his hand into his breeches pocket, apparently to take out a knife . . .

Well, Cobbett survived that election campaign and others, but his words remind us that this ' green and pleasant land ' has also, and always, had its struggles, its deep divisions, its violence and injustices. The golden meadows were golden only for a few and the pastoral rhapsodies of poets could not fill empty bellies.

The English countryside continued, as I'm sure it always will, to tempt its writers to explore and record their impressions of what they find. Each new pair of eyes will reveal something we may not see for ourselves.

George Borrow and John Keats were also two very keen travellers and both wrote about their wanderings in a way that has undoubtedly enriched our literature and our appreciation of the countryside. Borrow's *Wild Wales* still reads with a freshness that involves the reader in each excursion, and Keats's letters from his walking tour of the Lake District and Scotland are an amazing testimony of the enthusiasm of this slightly built, dying young poet from London.

"We proceeded from Ambleside to Rydal, saw the waterfalls there and called on Wordsworth, who was not at home, nor was any of his family. I wrote a note and left it on the mantelpiece. Thence, on we came to the foot of Helvellyn, where we slept, but could not ascend it for the mist . . . From Helvellyn we came to Keswick-on-Derwentwater. The approach to Derwentwater surpassed Windermere; it is richly wooded shut in with rich-toned mountains. From Helvellyn to Keswick was eight miles to breakfast, after which we took a complete circuit of the lake . . .

And all this before the age of cars, trains, or easy access to the country's beauty spots. Such travellers knew a quietness that we shall never know, for even if we get away from roads and railways there is the ever-increasing volume of traffic overhead.

One of the great advantages of a walking holiday, in all kinds of weather, is the intimate feeling you get with the landscape you are traversing. You get the smell of grass on your clothes and the earth sticks to your boots. You become 'one with nature'. "To enjoy a countryside," wrote the mountaineer F. S. Smythe, "it is essential to make a direct contact with it and this is only to be accomplished by walking over it."

Well, from before Chaucer's Pilgrims up to the present day, men and women have wanted to walk the countryside of Britain and twentieth-century man has not lost entirely the art of walking or writing about what he sees on his walks. John Hillaby's *Journey Through Britain* is a fine example. Despite all the pressures upon our countryside, the muddled planning, the spreading concrete and the wish of some to turn every quiet corner into an organized playground, we are still able to say with John Hillaby that "many parts of Britain are still inexpressibly beautiful. The sense of airy suspension, the racing cloud shadows of the Bredons, the Quantocks, and the Long Mynd, the sweep of the Pennine Way from Fountain Fell to Keld and the Border between Ettrick and Tweed contain contentment . . ." I think that is what most of us look for in nature—contentment. If you achieve *that*, I find that all other virtues and benefits follow.

There are, of course, several other twentieth-century writers one could quote from, both native and overseas. Was there ever a better 'writer of place'—in his letters as well as his novels—than D. H. Lawrence? Perhaps. H. M. Tomlinson,

Lawrence Durrell and Laurie Lee are just a trio of writers who can bring a new world to your armchair in the evocative way they each write about landscape. And what a pity that Tomlinson's work is so hard to find now.

Of the many overseas visitors to these islands I wonder if, in this century, anyone has written with greater charm and awareness of our landscape than the Chinese landscape artist Chiang Yee. In his book *The Silent Traveller* (published in 1937) he had this to say:

> Last summer I had the opportunity of visiting the Lakes and there I spent the most agreeable period of all my English experience. So happy was that stretch of time . . . I cannot analyse the peculiar beauty of those places . . . yet I was constantly aware of some half-likeable, half-melancholy strangeness . . . the clouds rising up from the valleys to the peaks, the mists hiding distant villages and tree-tops—all of these made me tireless of wandering and brought a great tranquillity of spirit.

Contentment and tranquillity of spirit may, then, be the only things we are really after when we set out on a journey; the destination, the getting there, doesn't always matter. If the journey itself is an interesting one it is easy to see what Robert Louis Stevenson meant when he said " To travel hopefully is a better thing than to arrive."

Half the fun of travelling for pleasure (rather than rushing from A to B) is to be found in the freedom you allow yourself for diversions—not those encountered on major roads when three miles is closed to patch up fifty yards, but those brought about by following your nose. "Adventure," wrote H. M. Tomlinson, "is never anywhere unless we make it. Chance releases it; some unexpected incidence of little things. The trouble is to know it in time, when we see it . . ."

I am aware that this chapter has become a small anthology of other people's thoughts about England over many years, but I make no apology for I hope they all show that there is always a great deal to learn about our own country, that it is a fascinating place and has been for at least 1,500 years. It will continue to be so only if we also help to keep its characteristics. "England," said George Santayana, "is the paradise of individuality, eccentricity, heresy, anomalies, hobbies and humours."

So I have called upon these many writers as witnesses in support of a perhaps unnecessary plea for a deeper appreciation of the land around us, the place where we live, the 'inexpressibly beautiful' corners where we can retreat to find contentment.

Dare I quote yet once more? Then let that fine essayist, William Hazlitt have almost the last word.

> One of the pleasantest things in the world is going on a journey; but I like to go by myself. I can enjoy Society in a room, but out of doors, nature is company enough for me . . . Give me the clear blue sky over my head, and the green turf beneath my feet, a winding road before me, and a three hours' march to dinner.

And on this question of whether one should travel abroad first, or in Britain, he has the perfect solution. " I should like well enough to spend the whole of my life in travelling abroad if I could anywhere borrow another life to spend afterwards at home!"

I know the feeling. I have just been reading a beautiful book on Italy and want to catch the next flight out of Heathrow. The art, the sculpture, the buildings, the cities, villages, the warmth, the wine and the people would be a marvellous refuge from an English winter. But, in a perverse way, I need a winter just as the land needs a good frost. I shall have to choose other signposts for my contentment. After all, roads and signposts, wherever they are, are all we need to begin an adventure. It would be a dull soul who could always ignore the appeal of either.

14

The End of a Season

I end as I began, by crossing the waters of the River Nene early in the morning and by going back to some of the places that these docile waters will have flowed through on their way to the fen country—Elton, Fotheringhay, Oundle.

In returning to Fotheringhay I was tempted to use the immortal words that Mary Queen of Scots had embroidered on her Chair of State—*In My End is My Beginning*—as the title for this chapter, for although I end these summer journeys where I began, they are but the beginning of a new awareness and love of the countryside in which I live.

Travelling round the counties of Cambridgeshire, parts of Lincolnshire, Norfolk and Northamptonshire, I have been reminded of many past joys and have discovered just as many new ones. When I walked out of my room that early April morning I had little idea of where I would be going or who I would be seeing within the area I had decided to re-explore. I was asked to write about this landscape in summer and I hope that those who prompted me won't be disappointed. It has certainly given me several very happy encounters and many enriching days. Now, as we come to the end of a season, I will return to my 'native' river for company.

The lime trees in the precincts have reached a perfection in dying. Their brief coronation turns into mourning. Their golden and amber leaves drop slowly, one by one, like a silent gun-salute. In *their* end is also their beginning as the summer begins to lie wet and limp at their feet.

The precincts are autumn-quiet. The mist hides the great stones but reveals the delicate cobwebs on bushes and trees. The grass is silver-plated with dew and hides now the summer footprints of all our visitors.

At the end of the town the river is motionless. I think it was John Baguley, my photographer, who was quoting a Greek proverb to me a few weeks ago which said "You can never jump into the same river twice." I'm sure that for most of the time this must be true, and yet I think you could jump into the same River Nene twice today because it appears frozen in its own silence. When I drop a dry stalk of grass on to its surface it stays there, as if dropped on to ice. It reminds me of that game we used to play as children, of getting a needle to float on a bowl of water.

Upstream, most of the boats have been moored for winter, their cabins locked, their awnings battened down for the last time this year. They have a forsaken look in the early morning light, like bathing-huts on a deserted sea-front, or children's swings in an empty park.

As the day brightens the water glistens but remains still. The river is empty not only of men in boats but also of swallows and martins. There are no swans either to be seen at the moment, and the heron is late for breakfast call.

The river stretches away beyond the developing and changing landscape around Peterborough, away into the Nene valley and Wansford, where the stone houses still seem to sleep, safe in the knowledge that for a little longer they are being allowed to remain in a village.

I rejoin the river at Elton, a favourite place of some hopes and several memories. The grass on the village green is long and wet. The chestnut trees, stripped by the boys of their conkers, stand shaken and bruised. The rusted leaves and the exploded shells lie scattered at the roots.

Any day now at Ashton, near Oundle, the Annual Conker Championship will be held. In recent years it has acquired an international status and has been called 'The World Conker Championship', with competitors taking part from South America, Spain, Germany and Australia. It's a day when men become boys again as they battle away through the eliminating contests, with their warrior-conkers on pieces of string. The village green will be crowded with spectators, there will be ancient rituals performed and refreshments at the local inn. It has all the fervour of jousting as the conkers crack, split, disintegrate and fall to the winner, and when it's over the R.N.I.B. will be about £100 better off.

I search in the long wet grass at Elton and find one conker that the boys have missed. I break open its spiky green armour and look with eyes of wonder at the bright, wet, shining, piebald nut that emerges, as lovely as a new-born foal. I put it in my pocket for a keepsake, knowing too well that within days it will have dried and begun to shrivel. But for the moment it is as precious as a diamond.

I cross the cattle-grid and pass the mill. I can hear the water spilling through the lock; I cross over, and walk along the now deserted path. The fields which have had crops have already been ploughed. The meadows are a green suede, brushed by the mist. The water is thick with weeds. Beyond the trees to my left is the village church, with its dignified tower, and Elton Hall—the seat of the Proby family. The Hall was originally built in the fifteenth century but rebuilt in the seventeenth and altered appreciably in the centuries that followed. It has not been open to the public now for a few years but I can remember summer afternoon teas there on the terrace, and cricket matches nearby—as a visitor, of course.

The path bends slightly and there, in the distance, is that magical view again of Fotheringhay church. It never fails to make the walk worthwhile and I stand for some time to enjoy both the scene and the silence. It is so still the leaves dare not fall from their trees but spin inaudibly on invisible threads.

I walk back to the green and the safe, stone houses of Main Street before taking the narrow road to Fotheringhay.

The day becomes warm and golden. The creeper on cottages grows scarlet. The reflections of the church in the river are as clear as they've been all summer. A group of children are playing on the mound where the castle once stood and a head was chopped off; and on this side of the river sheep graze contentedly in a field. How easily Nature can smooth the rough edges of history.

Elton, Fotheringhay, Tansor and Cotterstock. What a lovely chime of names to lead you into the ancient town of Oundle with its streets of solid, grey houses. After the towns in the lowlands of Cambridgeshire Oundle appears to be built on a hillside, especially at night when its lights draw you in out of the cold. The church has one of the finest and most elegant spires in Northamptonshire and it can be seen from several miles away, particularly when approached from the east.

Having taken evening classes in Oundle during long, dark winter months, my abiding memories of the town are of it at night when, after a fourteen-mile drive through fog, rain or snow, I have been grateful to see its lights sprinkled on the gentle slopes that rise from the River Nene. There are good inns in Oundle where you will find blazing fires to greet you plus good ale and food to comfort you.

But at the end of summer these are not yet needs to preoccupy your thoughts on arrival. On a mellow afternoon the stone buildings look warm and sleepy, and a stranger could be forgiven for thinking that he had arrived at a Cotswold town. Many of the shops have been able to retain their individuality and anyone looking for books, antiques, or fine prints will not be at a loss for an hour or two.

Inevitably much of Oundle's life and reputation revolves around its well-known school which began its life as far back as the fourteenth century as a small grammar school attached to the Guild of Our Lady of Oundle. After the Dissolution the school almost went out of existence through lack of money until one of its former pupils, Sir William Laxton, came to the rescue with plans for maintaining and improving the school. It continued to grow in size and prestige, until it became one of the finest schools for boys in the country. The chapel contains some of the first stained-glass windows designed by John Piper, who was to create that greater and very exciting window in Coventry Cathedral.

*   *   *

Any road out of Oundle takes you into a benevolent landscape of sloping fields, woods and unspoilt villages—Stoke Doyle, Wadenhoe and Aldwincle; or Barnwell, Thurning and Luddington; or Glapthorn, Southwick and Apethorpe.

Wadenhoe is an exceptionally satisfying discovery with good houses, attractive cottages, a church, pub and ford, all by the banks of the prettiest stretch of the Nene you could possibly find. The meadows are sweet and golden in spring with cowslips; kingfishers come here to make their nests; and the summer air is of a vintage one only associates with childhood or some dreamy nostalgia of a rural England long before noise and machinery came to rob us of peace. And yet a memorial tablet in the church will tell you that violence came to the lives of Wadenhoe people back in 1824, even though the act took place far away in Italy. Thomas Welch Hunt, the local squire, had married Caroline Isham of Polebrook and they decided on an Italian honeymoon. After a short stay in Rome they went to see the ruined temples near Paestum but they were attacked by bandits, shot, robbed, and died from their wounds. The full story is told in Sir Gyles Isham's own account of the tragedy in *Northamptonshire Past and Present*, the journal that has done so much to record the county's life.

Beyond Wadenhoe is the village of Aldwincle where the poet John Dryden was born on 9 August 1631 in the rectory, which was the home of his grandparents. Not much is known of him, though it seems that he spent most of his childhood at Tichmarsh before being sent to Westminster School. At the age of nineteen he went up to Trinity College, Cambridge, and from there to London, where he enjoyed considerable success as a poet, dramatist, critic and prose-writer. His translation of Virgil alone is said to have earned him £1,200. He became poet laureate in 1667 and was a much sought-after figure in London's coffee houses. He occasionally returned to Northamptonshire to visit relatives and to enjoy some fishing or a game of bowls. He died in May 1700 and was buried in Westminster Abbey, in Chaucer's grave.

One of the better-known villages of Northamptonshire is Barnwell, the home for several years now of the Duke and Duchess of Gloucester. It was once described as " a considerable town " with two parish churches, a castle, a weekly market, a fair, and a railway station. Now it is a quiet hamlet whose main attraction is ' the big house '. The little station disappeared three years ago and for most of the time Barnwell enjoys a quiet existence in very pastoral surroundings.

I take the narrow road that rises over the fields until I come to Thurning and Luddington. Suddenly I am aware of an exceptional stillness and feel that I am on a road that must be walked. There are wide grass verges and thick hedgerows abundant with berries, red and black.

I walk for about a mile until I come into woodland. The atmosphere is old and powerful. The sweet woodland smell makes me stop and drink of it, as if I have come to drink of some healing spring of water. How easily we forget these rich

smells of nature; the smell of newly ploughed earth; the smell of
hedgerows after rain; the smell of woodlands and their undergrowth. It is a sensation that reawakens old memories of what
it was like, hundreds of years ago, before frozen foods, before
car fumes and our molly-coddling alienation from the elements.
Do we inherit our ancestors' memories, I wonder? When we
stand on a piece of ground where we know we have never stood
before and yet feel convinced that we have definitely stood
there, is there some spirit in our bones that recognizes it for us?
I feel I have known these woods a long time, and yet I am sure
this is the first time I have stood beside them.

All the trees are still but for the aspens. Their leaves are
trembling with the sound of a slow, continual shower of rain.
The movement is fascinating but the sound even more so. I
am reminded of the lines from Edward Thomas's poem about
aspens—

> . . . it would be the same were no house near.
> Over all sorts of weather, men, and times,
> Aspens must shake their leaves and men may hear
> But need not listen . . .

In the still-stubbled fields beyond the trees fat pheasants are
gleaning, lapwings are holding parliament, and a lark sings as
brightly as it would on any spring morning. On the grass verge
the pink herb-robert is still in flower and toadstools shine like
ice-cream cornets. As the sun begins to drift towards the
horizon the sky has an apricot glow that changes the colour of
the earth.

Luddington, Hemington, Polebrook and Ashton bring me
back down to the banks of the River Nene at Oundle and, as I
take the road back to Fotheringhay, I tell myself that
Northamptonshire is a very *English* county, not demonstrative,
but genuine; not spectacular but rich in history and scenery.
Admittedly I have not been looking at its industrial areas or its
dull towns, I have not been thinking of Kettering, or Corby,
Wellingborough, or Northampton itself. But in its rural regions
there is undoubtedly much to admire and the villages I have
seen today are certainly the places that give the River Nene the
charm it needs to compete with the Great Ouse or the
Welland.

Fotheringhay, Nassington, Yarwell and Wansford, " and the

sun of October summery on the hill's shoulder ", as Dylan
Thomas described it in one of his poems. But I ought not to be
quoting a Welsh poet now for I am entering Clare country and
John Clare could describe this season as well as anyone.

> Autumn comes laden with her ripened load
> Of fruitage and so scatters them abroad
> That the fern-smothered heath and mole-hill waste
> Are black with bramble berries.

In writing about Northamptonshire I should, I know, devote
several pages to its most natural and gifted writer, but I have
written about Clare in each of my previous books and must
resist the temptation to say too much about him in this one.
John Clare and Northamptonshire are, nevertheless, synony-
mous for lovers of this countryside and Clare's position in
English letters now owes no small debt to the landscape of his
native county. I'm not sure what he would say if he were to
come back now and find that Helpston, the village of his birth,
had been moved into Cambridgeshire. Clare is not a lowlands
poet but one of the woods, heaths and commons of
Northamptonshire. Few writers have been so aware of their
roots, so aware of their surroundings. He was influenced by this
countryside and its people from his earliest years and he
became an interpreter of what this land had to say. In one of
his poems he wrote

> I felt that I'd a right to song
> And sung—but in a timid strain—
> Of fondness for my native plain . . .

Well, the timid strain has lasted for over 150 years and he is
still one of the most important sources of natural history for the
county. No one had a keener eye for what is to be seen in the
countryside, and his poetry teaches us also how to *see*.

As the River Nene sweeps down through the generous Nene
Valley it passes through a fine landscape that Clare would
have known. Not far off the A47 are several minor roads that
take you into the heart of Clare's landscape. Southorpe,
Barnack, Upton, Ailsworth and Castor Hanglands. This was
also Roman territory and many valuable discoveries have been
made around the village of Castor, particularly at Durobrivae,
the best-known Roman town in the whole area, which was

excavated by John Clare's friend, Edmund Artis, who was Steward to the Earl Fitzwilliam over 150 years ago. Durobrivae was a wealthy centre in Roman times and a recent discovery of Roman–Christian silver proved to be of international importance.

The A47 dips down from Castor Hill to Milton Ferry, which was a natural beauty spot of some years ago with a lovely walk through the Lynch to the village of Alwalton, but now, alas, no more!

Another mile or two and twentieth-century Peterborough draws you like a spider into its web of ring-roads, roundabouts, lights and traffic. But, before it does, there is one ancient monument that is worth visiting and that is the Longthorpe Tower, built in the early part of the fourteenth century and of particular interest in recent years because of the remarkable wall-paintings discovered at the end of the Second World War. The paintings had been hidden under several coats of limewash and distemper, and it was only when the tenant Mr Hugh Horrell was preparing to redecorate the rooms, after the Tower had been vacated by the Home Guard, that the paintings were revealed.

The guide-book tells us that "no comparable scheme of domestic mural decoration of such completeness and of this early date exists in England, and very few upon the Continent . . ." Certainly to stand in the Great Chamber before such a display of fine wall-paintings is an exciting experience. The Nativity Scene, The Seven Ages of Man, and the Wheel of Life are scenes you can take with you into the busy streets of today.

*   *   *

An ancient and traditional event, which is also a reminder that we have reached the end of a season, is the Peterborough Bridge Fair and I get the feeling that before the night is out I shall succumb to its noise and bright lights.

The earliest of the Peterborough fairs was called the Patermas Fair, or St Peter's Fair, after the patron saint of the abbey. They were, to begin with, held within the Minster Precincts before being moved outside the abbey gates and on to the market square. The first charter granted to the Abbot was

signed by Richard I on 24 March 1189, just before the King set
off for the Holy Land. The granting of charters for fairs and
markets was, in fact, a fund-raising exercise to help finance the
crusades. A second charter was also granted to the Abbot to
hold a St Oswald's Fair during the eight days following the
second Sunday in Lent. But the fair that really prospered and
survived with at least some of its old traditions was the
Peterborough ' Brigge Fair ', established in 1439 by a charter
which was granted to the abbey by Henry VI. Originally the
fair was held on 20–22 September, but later changed to the
first Tuesday–Thursday of October. The opening of the fair
was always an important event in the city and special prayers
were said at the morning service in the cathedral. These were
followed by a civic proclamation and a sausage lunch. Like
many fairs the Bridge Fair had strong ties with a feast day and
pork became the meat traditionally served at Peterborough
Roasting-pigs were bred specially for the week and were
known as ' Bridge-fairers '. Roast pork sizzled in the booths,
the stall-holders sold pork-pies, sausages, tripe and faggots. A
lot of drinking went on too and, with so much beer and liquor
about, the fair also earned the reputation of being the
drunkards' fair. It frequently had another name too, ' The
Mud Fair ', for the low meadows by the Nene on which the fair
was held used to flood in wet weather, and Bridge Fair weather
is notoriously wet. In its more prosperous days the fair was held
on both sides of the river and as far down as London Road.
The main streets of the city also had extra stalls and the local
shops remained open to compete for all the extra money
flowing into the town from the thousands of visitors. When the
railways came to Peterborough there were a few heated
arguments about the siting of the stations and tracks so as not
to interfere with the ancient fairs' rights to use land on both
sides of the river, but in the end it was the railways that helped
the fairs to prosper for a few more years. In 1859 the L. and
N.W. Railway brought 2,500 visitors; the Great Eastern
brought 2,400; the Great Northern 3,000; and the Midland
1,500—no mean influx of spending power in those days,
especially coming so soon at the end of the harvest when people
had a bit of extra money to spend. And it must be remembered
that the fairs in those days were not just for amusement, they
were also great trading posts. The fairs were, as one old horse-

keeper in the fens told me " a time for getting yourself set up for winter—boots, trousers, tools, smocks and other bits and pieces." They were great gathering places for horsemen and farm-labourers generally. Farmers frequently sent their work-men in to the fair on wagons decorated with laurels, flowers and evergreens. At its peak the fair saw some extensive trading carried on around all the entertainments, drinking and merry-making. Horses, cattle, sheep, timber, wool, coopers' wares, cheeses, pies, pots and earthenware were always in demand. In 1864 " 5,000 beast, 700 horses, 180 sheep and 75 rams " were sold in three days. There are still several people in the area who can remember buying horses at Bridge Fair, as Mrs Dow's father did, for instance, when he bought their family pony there for £8 just before the First World War. All such trading now, of course, has disappeared and the old spirit has gone too. What we have in its place are the hot-dogs, hamburgers, candy-floss and ' just a lot of electrical gadgets '.

Although the fairs have declined and become more tawdry, their early importance cannot be overlooked. They gave a town status and helped towards the growth of the city we know today. People no longer come in their train-loads or on decorated wagons, and there are very few people who are now able to live in the centre of the city to feel that they belong to the city's traditions. When the heart goes out of a city much of its natural life goes too; the continuity is broken, the magic dispelled.

But at least the Bridge Fair is back again and it was officially opened today with all the traditional civic recognition and launching it deserves. By darkness thousands of coloured lights splashed into the sky, ten changes of colour every second, to accompany the screams, thrills, shouts and laughter of people who can't resist the crazy, unreal world of fairs.

I can't resist them and have loved them since I was a child. It was always a great thrill to be taken out into the dark streets and up to the market place of my home town of Whittlesey to where the familiar spaces had been filled with golden round-abouts, steam horses, swing-boats and roll-a-penny. The ' Rock King ', with his waxed moustache and straw hat, made yards of coloured rock ' before your very eyes ' and piled his stall high with glistening boiled sweets that made your eyes stick out like chapel hat-pegs and your tongue thirst for a taste of those sweet jewels from his sticky casket. The noise, the smells, the whirling and thrilling, the transformation of our ordinary world, is something I shall never forget. And then to be taken home for bed and to hear the sounds still drifting over the moonlit rooftops of the town to my small bedroom. I've forgotten what prizes I won, if any, but the fair gave us something to talk about for weeks.

I made my way over the bridge tonight with all those who would not leave until they'd had a go at everything—the darts, hoop-la, coconuts, roll-a-penny, win-a-goldfish, the hot-dogs, hamburgers, candy-floss, toffee-apples, " and now let's go on the Big Wheel!"

But do fairs really have the magic that they once had? I must admit after the initial excitement of entering the ground tonight the magic soon faded for me. The noise and glare, the smells and stalls were there, but something was missing. I watched the bright, six-pointed star of the Big Wheel spinning like an illuminated windmill against the black sky; I watched the youngsters enjoying themselves on the Cyclone, the Flying Coaster, the Ben Hur, the Fly-In, the Dodgems and the Cakewalk, but underneath the brilliant, gaudy lights, underneath the avalanche of noise and jungle of smells, the old atmosphere of the fair had gone. The side-stalls were neglected. Stall-holders waited patiently for people to try their luck at winning teddybears or plastic toys. There were no side-shows, no barkers drumming up an audience to see sword-swallowers, fire-eaters, fattest ladies, fourth-rate striptease dancers, all-in wrestlers or doubtful boxing champions. No two-headed pigs or mice, no bearded princesses or grotesque dwarfs; the oddities of this world were more likely to be seen walking round the amusements as customers or competitors rather than performers. The striped awnings of the tents no longer held a secret or forbidden world, no longer had any mystery or furtive joy. The amusements have now entered the space age and give you ' trips to the moon ' or ' journey to the unknown ' for 40p; or they have died out altogether and have become as extinct as the naphtha flame or original dancing bear. I didn't see anyone win a coconut, or shoot down a ping-pong ball from a jet of water, or knock out the heavyweight. But, none the less, everybody appeared to be enjoying themselves in their own way and chewed happily at their hot-dogs and onions as they were fired into space for a minute or two. The fairground people on the whole looked disillusioned, fed up and dumb, as if they have at last lost any enthusiasm for their tradition. They let their amplifiers make a noise for them, and this fiercesome row screamed like a raw protest against the silence of the night.

Back in the quiet precincts I acknowledge, with a grateful heart, that moment in history when the Abbot decided that the time had come for the fair to be held outside the abbey gates. Now I can spend the last two hours of the day silently recording all those impressions I have tried to store briefly in the memory with the other half-waking memories of other years. I can still see in my mind the mirror-still river, the hibernating boats, the threadbare chestnut trees, the stone cottages, the quivering aspen leaves, the Big Wheel, and the ghost of the old Rock King. The words try but cannot do the day justice. I light a lamp and begin to read Kilvert's *Diaries*. What a lovely and infectious sense of humour he had. What a delightful man he must have been to know. How naturally he relates the everyday incidents and conversation of his parishioners. He can move with compassion and provoke mirth in one paragraph.

Dryden, Clare, Kilvert, and many others, all room-mates under the same roof, all brought together to share a summer journey! The room vibrates with them, and yet, before that previous tenant scratched his name upon my window-pane in 1886, all three were dead.

> The bells tell of midnight,
> dark petals of sound
> falling on the table of silence
> in this ancient house.
>
> I, like John Clare, have moved
> to another home in middle-years
> and have not been alone
> in expecting miracles.
>
> On my window an earlier tenant
> scratched his name and the date,
> believing that eighteen-eighty-six
> had some significance.

Now, in nineteen-seventy-seven,
I am reminded of him for whom
walls were just walls
when unshared by his love.

But I will keep sane, I will
give thanks for the stones.
Too many names scratched on the glass
will obscure the view.

*   *   *

These early autumn days (as so often happens) are warmer and brighter than many of the days we have had during summer. People are still around in summer dresses and open-neck shirts; the cameras are still clicking away, capturing those coloured moments to project proudly on some cold winter evening when friends call; the streets still have something of a festive atmosphere and we are all eagerly trying to prolong the days as much as possible. Only the slow shower of yellow leaves gives the season away. Autumn must be to a road-sweeper what Christmas is to a postman—a losing battle, until the last leaf is delivered to the winter's door-mat and the branches can no longer answer.

It is too great a temptation to stay indoors. The columns of the cathedral shine like glass, the grass shimmers like water, and the sky beckons. I feel that I want to see again in just one day all that I have seen in a whole season. I want rivers, fields, fens and forests; I want the sea, the Nature Reserves, the farms and country kitchens where I have sat for many hours talking to people who know the land better than I. But it is too late for the harvest fields and the summer flowers, too late for daydreaming on Woodwalton Fen or picnicking in Norfolk. All that is left for me now is a day's blackberrying and a few warm hours along the autumn hedgerows. It's a pursuit I shall follow with contentment for I have good memories of blackberry picking in many parts of the country—on Whinlatter Pass in Cumbria, on the cliffs of North Devon and the Ridgeway in Berkshire, and in the lanes of Suffolk and Norfolk. But blackberrying along the hedgerows I have known for a lifetime makes all the difference. It's like picking fruit out of your own garden. The hedgerows are also a harvest of summers and, when you listen to the skylarks singing, they too are the descendants of earlier generations who have been part of this landscape. Even the distant church bells at the weekend have a familiarity which encourages this feeling of 'belonging to a place'.

And so, back to Elton, Nassington, Yarwell and Wansford, back to Southorpe, Barnack, Ufford and Helpston. The berries may not be as fat and tasty as those at Denver or Guist, but they will be from hedgerows that John Clare would have known and this year's crop has its own blessing.

> They almost ask to be picked.
> Their faces shining eagerly
> on begging briars, as if
> summer had ripened them too soon
> and autumn frightened them with thoughts
> far darker than their juice.
>
> The lapwings squeak like chalk.
> The empty harvest fields
> have smells full of nostalgia.
> The sun's last warmth
> falls with the sound of bells
> from Wansford, Yarwell and Nassington.
>
> It is fitting for a marriage of seasons
> to have such ceremony.
> The berries falling into my jar
> are both a sacrifice and vow.
> Today I take, absorb, and bless earth's ringing parishes.

And the jars ooze with summer, with hours of sunlight and warmth. When the berries become pie or jam they will still taste of these picking days.

After a few hours of fighting with some of the higher briars for those unattainable prize clusters that always stay beyond reach, I decide to drive away from the hedgerows into the open fens where to find a blackberry is like finding a Roman coin in mint condition.

Here the hedgerows have mostly disappeared and the unfenced fields have little to offer to bird or man, but I go to be back again in the great spaces that the fens present with even greater intensity in these blue and gold days of October.

I find myself retracing the course of the Old River Nene, sometimes called the Medieval River Nene, which is vastly different from that of today. In former times the river took a considerable loop south of Peterborough, passing near to Farcet and Yaxley, Whittlesea Mere, Holme and Ramsey. It then turned north-east through Ramsey Mere and on to Benwick, March and Upwell. There were also several very ancient artificial waterways in the fens long before Vermuyden started his work in the seventeenth century. Field-study of recent years has proved that many of these dykes existed in Roman times and were used by them for transporting cargoes to different parts of the region.

When I get to March I turn back and take the road over West Fen to The Turves. At Beggar's Bridge I walk along the bank of Twenty Foot River (one of those great straight drains cut in 1651) and look over those enormous fields. Did the Roman Legions once have a trackway over these to Coates, Eldernell and Thorney? There is certainly a feeling of great antiquity about the region today.

I turn in the opposite direction and make my way down to Burnt House and Whittlesey Dyke. The continents of clouds above me are making their own history. The sky deepens. The sun is getting near to the horizon. Lapwings fight in a nearby field. A hare leaps along the riverbank and into a heap of potatoes. The water shines cold as steel. The silence again is frightening, overpowering and immense. If you try to shout it pushes the words back down your throat. If you try to clap your hands it wedges itself between your palms and deadens the sound. From Burnt House I drive along Cock Bank and call again to see Geoffrey Armstrong at work in his barn. Today he is busy polishing a marvellous specimen of black bog oak, black as soot and nearly as hard as coal. It's many thousands of years old but is taking a new life under this sculptor's hands. The light is failing for us both and I do not stay very long.

I follow the course of Bevill's Leam along Glassmoor Bank to Pondersbridge and Farcet Fen. There are hundreds of starlings congregating on some nearby telegraph-wires. They are so tightly packed together that their weight makes the wires sag like heavy black cables. They make a few flurries of flight before the whole flock suddenly swirls off like a dark blizzard in that strange sunset ritual of theirs before finally scattering to roost.

Suddenly a blinding light floods across the fens, coating everything in brilliant gold. The fields, the rivers, the grass and the windows of houses, blaze with a power that goes beyond excitement and becomes terrifying. Any moment now the world must catch fire or explode. The sky's light is too fierce to behold. I wait for the earth to melt and flow into space. But then the sun surrenders to the horizon and fades quickly into a silent nothingness. The rivers, the cattle, the fields and farms are all restored and I return home under a darkening heaven with stars as crisp as autumn leaves.

And so another summer ends, a season is over; I put on the early evening lights and sit by the fire in a room that has known 250 summers before.

I sit waiting for an owl to call from a nearby garden but know that tonight its call will not be heard. I have listened all summer to its nocturnal fluting but the postman told me this morning that he had found the owl dead at the foot of a tree with its wings broken. It's like waiting for the hourly chimes of a clock that you know will never strike again. There is an emptiness and silence that is final.

15

Late Gatherings

After a few days of early fog and wintry mornings the sun of St Luke's little summer suddenly appears again and the early October days are once more bright with clear light, with sharp blue skies and a welcome warmth. They have also given me the added bonus of a few late gatherings, bringing together a few last impressions before the autumn finally takes over.

Yesterday, for instance, I went to see Mr and Mrs Dow again and found them already planning for the winter months, with enough activities to keep them busy for a whole year— patchwork quilts, shopping-bags, handbags and curtains.

"What do you use when you go shopping?" asked Mrs Dow.

"Well . . ." and here I hesitated, because I am not the world's most organized shopper . . . "I sometimes have a plastic carrier-bag or I just hope that the things I buy will fit into my pockets; why?"

She shook her head. "You can't go shopping like that, not with a plastic carrier. Here, you'd better have this!" And she gave me a hand-made tweed shopping-bag that she'd just finished, complete with inside pockets for stamps, letters, and, as she pointed out, "your pension book when the time comes".

I also called to see Mr Sam Briggs, who was preparing for a journey to Yorkshire to stay with his daughter until Christmas, and we strolled down his garden path to enjoy the sunlight. The long garden was tidy, the late crops looked healthy, and my admiration for this ninety-two-year-old grew as I saw with what pride he still went about his work, pulling up a weed he had missed before, brushing back some soil he had knocked on to the path.

And last night I had a long talk with an eighty-one-year-old fen farmer who had worked on the land all his life, labouring for his father for two shillings a week until he was old enough to rent his own farm.

" I've known us leave home at half-past three in the morning for a day's hay-making and not get 'um until ten o'clock at night. The hired hands got eleven bob a week but us ol' boys got two, plus our keep."

" Did you grumble about it?"

" What were the point when you worked for your father? He had twelve children, eight boys and four girls, so he was on the right side—he bred his own farm-hands. When I were an ol' boy at school I used to have to get up half an hour earlier to go and do some jobs for my auntie, y'know—chop the fire-wood, get the coal in, empty the slops, things like that, and she'd give me a ha'penny . . . Do you know why I've got a deformed spine? It's from carrying eighteen-stone sacks of corn on my back from when I was a boy. Harvesting, potato-lifting, beet-chopping, twitch-pulling, I've done the lot."

" What were the summers like then?"

" The same as they are now. Some hot, some wet, some indifferent. I've gathered in the harvest by boat when the fields have been flooded and I've passed-out from the heat of the sun 'cus it were so hot. Some summers were so hot we used to get our first beer-break at eight o'clock in the morning. But I liked harvest-work, there was something special about it and every-body took an interest . . ."

They were memories I'd heard several times before in different houses and from different people, from my own family and from strangers, and there was a bitter-sweet taste in the telling.

*   *   *

The trees are clinging to their last leaves like possessive parents reluctant to lose their children. The days smell of bonfires, the nights speak of frosts, and the sun now struggles to rise above the grey stones of the cathedral. The yew tree is permanently in shadow. Daybreak arrives later each morning and the lights go on sooner in the evening. The paper-boy hurries his round, delivering the latest headlines—the news of today's world events, political arguments, agreements, disagreements, strikes, settlements, fires, deaths, royal babies and summit meetings.

Which of our headlines will be remembered or relevant in fifty or a hundred years' time?

The choristers assemble for rehearsals—schoolboys on bikes and arguing about football and comics. They enter the Song School, begin to sing, eventually emerge fully robed and pliant, transformed into angelic sounds that will be heard not only in the cathedral but on broadcast Evensong and on long-playing records of religious music. For some of them this summer will be part of history and they will return in many years to come, as some of their predecessors do, men who were choristers here fifty and sixty years ago.

* * *

I am aware that in writing about the summer months and memories of certain places that I may have been momentarily blind to what is really happening now. During the last few days I have, for instance, read of the plans to build a nuclear power station at Denver, and the thought appals me. Not only is a lovely corner of East Anglia threatened but thousands of acres of farmland will be lost for ever and this gentle landscape ruined. It's not only the building of a nuclear power station but all that goes with it. The effects of North Sea oil on parts of Scotland is a typical example. More traffic, greater demands for amenities, more noise and fiercer pressures on the local environment, all producing rapid changes. Whether the nuclear power station comes or not, new roads will be made from the Midlands to the east coast, new towns will be built, more farms and cottages will disappear. Farmyards that I walked through at the beginning of this year are already under concrete, and you can't help feeling that you have been part of a summer that never can return. People are leaving the land. Cottages are deserted. Rooms and abandoned chairs are empty. Are the roots withering? Have we finally rejected the soil?

The last days of summer pass. The roads become black again with the greasy mud of an early winter. The ooze of sugar-beet lorries begins to mix with the mist of November until we have the familiar fenland sludge of unsweetened treacle on grass verges and pavements. Depressed skies once again begin to press down on the houses, putting early shutters on windows, making the streets stiller than silence. Every light now emphasizes the power of distance. But inside those homes the wood-fires are burning, kettles are singing on the hobs or whistling in kitchens. The talk of the people is, I know, as warm as blood, sweeter than newly dug parsnips, and there the heart truly *feels* at home.

You cannot refuse, or ignore, these feelings that say you are *home*, that you are where the roots are, that you are where you belong. In my Introduction to this book I spoke of my doubts, about not wanting to write again about this landscape, and how I changed my mind. "I went out because I could not ignore the season . . . And the mist moved away / Leaving the fields shining innocently under the sun."

Well, my friendly critic, you asked me why I seldom wrote about summer in the fens and these new pages may, or may not, give you an answer. At least let me say how grateful I am to you for the prompting because the last few months have given me many moments of pleasure and much to think about. Now I close the shutters, draw the curtains, put on the lights, pull a chair up to the fire and settle down once more for winter. A year ago I had no idea that this book would be written and perhaps next year I shall go back to some of the ideas that your suggestion made me put to one side for a while. I'm not sorry and I hope that you will at last be able to convince your friends in other parts of the country that you do not have to live in an igloo all the year round.

The most appropriate words I can find with which to conclude this journal come from a poem by Robert Frost, called 'Reluctance'.

> Out through the fields and the woods
>   And over the walls I have wended;
> I have climbed the hills of view
>   And looked at the world, and descended;
> I have come by the highway home,
>   And lo, it is ended
>
> The leaves are all dead on the ground,
>   Save those that the oak is keeping
> To ravel them one by one
>   And let them go scraping and creeping
> Out over the crusted snow,
>   When others are sleeping.

And the dead leaves lie huddled and still,
 No longer blown hither and thither;
The last lone aster is gone;
 The flowers of the witch-hazel wither;
The heart is still aching to seek,
 But the feet question ' Whither?'

Ah, when to the heart of man
 Was it ever less than a treason
To go with the drift of things,
 To yield with a grace to reason,
And bow and accept the end
 Of a love or a season?

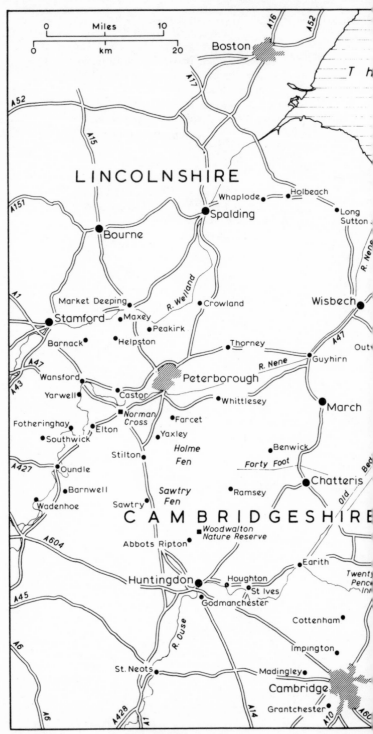

Based, with permission, on the Ordnance Survey

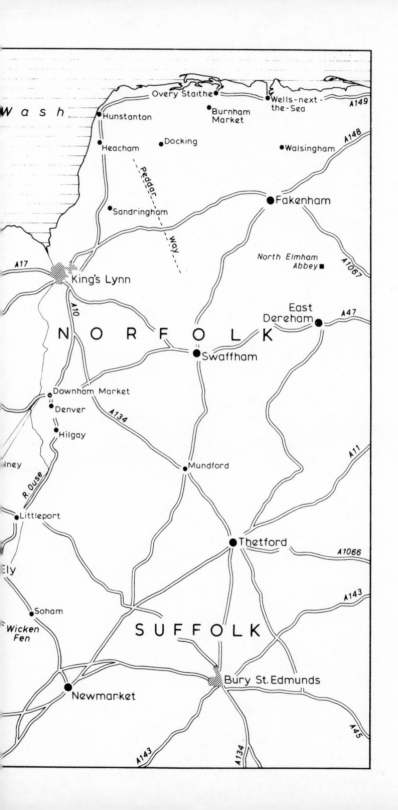

Index